Oregon's Joseph Branch: History Through the Miles

Barton Jennings

Oregon's Joseph Branch: History Through the Miles
Copyright © 2019 by Barton Jennings

Publisher's Cataloging-in-Publication Data
Jennings, Barton

Oregon's Joseph Branch: History Through the Miles
146p.; 21cm.
ISBN: 978-1-7327888-1-7

Library of Congress Control Number: 2019904820

First Edition

Cover photos by Barton Jennings, Ed Spaulding – front cover (courtesy of the Friends of the Joseph Branch) and Sarah Jennings – back cover

Please send comments or corrections to sarah@techscribes.com

TechScribes, Inc.
PO Box 620
Avon, IL 61415
www.techscribes.com

Printed in the United States of America

This May 2004 special charter train, shown at Joseph, was the reason for the first draft of this book. Photo by Barton Jennings.

Other books by this author:

Arkansas & Missouri Railroad: History Through the Miles
Alaska Railroad: History Through the Miles
Iowa Interstate Railroad: History Through the Miles
Everett Railroad: History Through the Miles
Tennessee Central Railway: History Through the Miles
Whitewater Valley Railroad: History Through the Miles

Contents

Preface

The historic Joseph Branch was built in a time of optimism and has survived several movements to abandon most of the line. For years, it was essentially invisible except for its few shippers and the crews that kept it operating. It was sold in the 1990s and then began to face the possibility that parts of the line would be abandoned, never seeing another train again. However, some of the railroad may have become even more famous as excursion trains returned to parts of the line. These trips have been operating since 2003, and today the Eagle Cap Excursion Train operates a number of regular and themed trips out of their new station in Elgin, Oregon.

This route description was first written in 2003-2004 for several charter trips that the author operated over the railroad from Joseph to Gulling and back on May 22-23, 2004. With updated information, and the many changes that have happened since the charter trains, the route description has been updated and added to. Much of the information comes from internal railroad records, government and public records, railroad workers, and conversations with old and new friends. Some of the information comes from the author's own personal notes from a time when he managed the maintenance of the line. It is hoped that you enjoy your adventure with Oregon's Joseph Branch. Hopefully this book will be of assistance in some ways – Oregon's Joseph Branch: History Through the Miles.

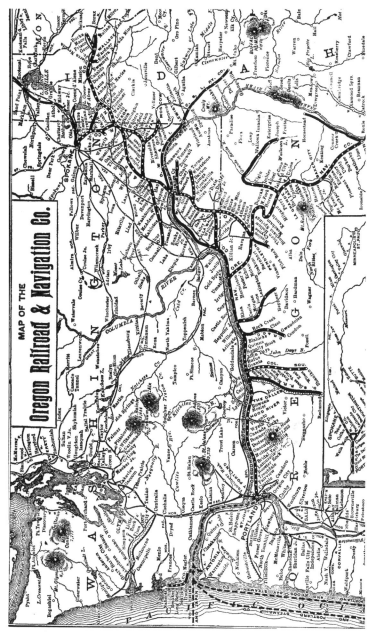

Map of the Oregon Railroad & Navigation Co. from the January 1910 edition of The Official Guide of the Railways and Steam Navigation Lines of the United States.

7

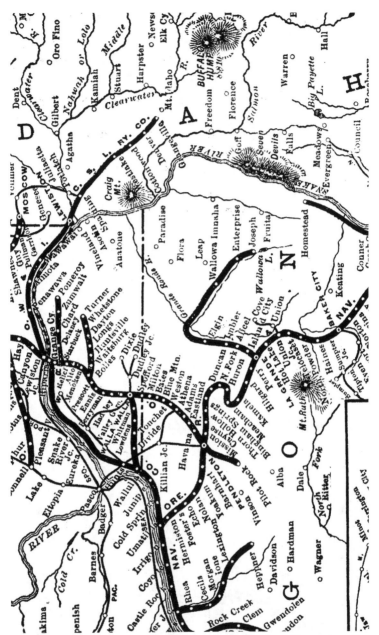

Enlarged portion of Map of the Oregon Railroad & Navigation Co. from the January 1910 edition of The Official Guide of the Railways and Steam Navigation Lines of the United States.

History of the Joseph Branch

The former Union Pacific Joseph Branch is one of those lines that somehow falls into the category of a legend. Maybe it is because it was built in an area of enormous beauty, but where few actually traveled. Maybe it was because the line seemed to just stick out on the maps, being surrounded by a large blank area. Whatever the reason, the line has an interesting history.

The line was originally built up the Grande Ronde Valley between La Grande and Elgin in 1890 by the **Oregon Railway Extension Company**. The Oregon Railway Extension Company was incorporated in Oregon on May 25, 1888, as a non-operating subsidiary of the **Oregon Railway and Navigation Company**, which had been created on June 13, 1879. The company built two rail lines. One line was from Winona to Seltice, Washington, a total of 47.84 miles. The second line is part of the Joseph Branch – 20.89 miles from La Grande to Elgin, Oregon. This initial line provided service to the large farming industry throughout the valley and also connected the valley to the timber industry at Elgin. North of Elgin, the country got very rugged and it wasn't until 15 years later that the line was extended.

On July 16, 1896, **The Oregon Railroad & Navigation Company** was chartered. A month later on August 17, 1896, the new company acquired the Oregon Railway Extension Company and its owner, the Oregon Railway & Navigation Company, under foreclosure. According to the Interstate Commerce Commission, the "property was operated by the Oregon Short Line Railway Company and its successor Oregon Short Line and Utah Northern Railway Company under lease as a part of the Oregon Railway and Navigation Company system, from the dates the sections of road were placed in operation to October 13, 1898, and from the latter date to date of sale by receivers."

The rugged mountains tower above the trains on the Joseph Branch, as demonstrated by this freight train in 1986. Photo by Barton Jennings.

About the same time in 1898, Union Pacific Railroad (UP) purchased a majority stake in the company, which became UP's gateway to the Pacific Northwest. With this acquisition and its accompanying financial power, the line was extended on to Joseph between 1905 and 1908 by The Oregon Railroad & Navigation Company. The construction of the line received some coverage in the national press. For example, the March 23, 1906, issue of *The Railway Age* reported that the Oregon Railroad & Navigation Company was building a line from "Elgin northeast up Grande Ronde River to the junction with the Wallowa River and thence southeast to Joseph, a total of 64 miles." At the time, 17 miles of grade was completed by the contractor George McCabe. George McCabe, and his brother A. J. McCabe, were in the lumber business, railroad construction business, and also leased and sold railroad equipment from their Portland,

Oregon, headquarters. *The Economist* of December 26, 1906, reported that "16.20 miles were completed, the grading was completed on 39.80 miles, and was progressing on the remaining 6.30 miles." Less than two years later, the line was completed.

The Grande Ronde and Wallowa Rivers provided most of the route of the Joseph Branch, shown here near Looking Glass. Photo by Barton Jennings.

By the early 1900s, most of the railroads in the northwest were being acquired by the consolidating systems of Northern Pacific, Great Northern, and Union Pacific. On November 23, 1910, the **Oregon–Washington Railroad & Navigation Company** was chartered under the general laws of Oregon to consolidate the many lines built. During the early 1900s, Union Pacific Chairman Judge Lovett, who took control of the railroad after E. H. Harriman's death in 1909, proposed the further consolidation of Union Pacific with its subsidiary roads. On May 10, 1932, UP stockholders approved the lease of the Oregon–Washington Railroad & Navigation Company, plus several other subsidiaries and railroads. The consolidation proposal went to the Interstate

Commerce Commission for approval almost immediately. At first, the proposal was denied on January 26, 1933, but was later approved on July 26, 1935, with a number of conditions, including acquiring several other connecting companies.

On January 1, 1936, the Oregon–Washington Railroad & Navigation Company was consolidated into Union Pacific. On that day, UP formally leased the railroad right-of-way and equipment of its subsidiaries, creating what was known as the Union Pacific System. Essentially, each subsidiary remained a company, its equipment, paychecks and other items still carrying its name, but Union Pacific operated all the railroads as one rail system. Because of bonding arrangements and other legal issues, many of these subsidiaries remained for more than fifty years. The railroad operated under the lease until December 30, 1987, when these leased companies were fully merged into the Union Pacific Railroad.

The completion of the line to Wallowa was celebrated with an excursion train from La Grande to Wallowa in 1908. According to the *News Record* of Enterprise, "Quite a crowd is expected, so eager are the people to see the famed beauty of the valley." In fact, between 1500 and 2000 people gathered with much fanfare, including several brass bands, to celebrate the arrival of the first passenger train. Ticket prices for the first train to Wallowa were $1.75. The line reached its maximum length in 1927 when the line was extended a short distance in Joseph to reach a new grain elevator.

Operations of the Joseph Branch

Between World War I and the Great Depression, the Joseph Branch was used extensively for hauling logs to local sawmills. During the booming 1920s, a dedicated daily passenger train served the line with a planned and advertised direct connection to and from Portland, Oregon. In 1926, the

Branch was covered by a daily passenger train (#42 to Joseph and #41 return) that was timed to connect to Trains #24 and #23 from and to Portland, Oregon.

The Great Depression and World War II changed this somewhat, as did the development of the personal automobile and a system of roads. By 1948, the Joseph Branch was part of Union Pacific's Idaho Division, which extended all the way west to La Grande. A daily except Sunday mixed train served the line as #304 eastward (toward Joseph) and #305 westward. This meant that any passengers were riding a freight train, often experiencing the delays required to switch customers along the line.

In 1948, the mixed train made a full round trip each day it ran, leaving La Grande at 7:00am and arriving at Joseph at 11:15am. It left Joseph at 12:45pm as #305 and got back to La Grande at 5:00pm, both trains taking 4 hours and 15 minutes for an average speed of 19.7 mph. The departure and arrival times at La Grande were convenient for local residents, but they meant a several hour wait after getting off eastbound train #18 at 4:57am or for westbound #17 at 9:00pm for movements from and to Portland. Eastbound connections were really bad, generally with about a six hour wait. This route guide will follow the progress of trains #304 and #305 throughout the route description, based upon the 1948 schedule.

Passenger trains #17 and #18 were the *Portland Rose*, a daily train operating Portland to Kansas City, running through to St. Louis under the operations of the Wabash Railroad. The trains also had direct connections to Seattle. They generally featured a number of sleeping cars, a club lounge plus a dining car, coaches, and a number of post office and baggage cars. The *Portland Rose* began service on September 12, 1930, as the top Union Pacific train to the Pacific Northwest, and operated until Amtrak took over on May 1, 1971. The trains were noted for being one of only two on the railroad to include its own, exclusive china pattern.

By August 1949, the Joseph Branch was part of the Oregon Division of Union Pacific. Mixed train service over the branch continued through the April 24, 1960, timetable, always found in Table 72 of the Union Pacific public timetable. The final schedule showed the train operating as #304 to Joseph daily except Saturday with the return train #305 operating daily except Sunday. The two trains operated separately (not as a daily round trip as done earlier) with them meeting somewhere between Elgin and Looking Glass. Actually the trains probably met at Elgin with Gulling being used as an alternative siding. Since the trains both operated as mixed trains and a great deal of business existed at Elgin, the rider probably had some time to see the sights while waiting at Elgin (look at the Elgin-Looking Glass travel times for #304 and #305 and see the large differences) for the La Grande-bound train to do its work.

During steam days, the Joseph Branch was limited to consolidation-type (2-8-0) locomotives. As diesel-electric locomotives took over, early GP-type locomotives generally handled the trains. Business on this line has always included three major items: lumber, grain and livestock. Sawmills have been located all along the line, primarily at La Grande, Elgin, Wallowa, Enterprise and Joseph. Grain elevators stood in almost every town, today generally labeled PGG (Pendleton Grain Growers) or Wallowa County Grain Growers. While most of the grain up here is wheat, other crops such as mint and grass seed are common. Livestock was also once a product moved over the line in some volume, as evidenced by the number of abandoned corrals along the railroad.

The 1970s were probably the last happy years on the Joseph Branch. Several major sawmills still operated, and trains could run full. In 1976, a local freight worked the line six days a week. Train #304 would depart La Grande at 9:00am on Sunday, Tuesday and Thursday, and get to Joseph during the early afternoon. The crew would take a rest, and was then scheduled to return the following day (Monday, Wednesday and Friday) as train #305. This train was scheduled to leave Joseph at 7:00am, and get to La Grande shortly after noon. However, freight volumes could greatly delay that arrival time.

During 1985-1986, the book's author was a Roadmaster for Union Pacific Railroad in La Grande. His territory included the Joseph Branch, as well as the mainline to Huntington. A few stories from that time period will be included in these notes. For example, during late February, 1986, a series of fast thaws and freezes caused a great deal of flooding along the line. Notes from the time show 15 specific locations where the track was either washed out, under water, or covered with a mudslide. It was such a big job that a special repair budget was created and it took several weeks to have the line all put back together. Also for your information, at that time the local on the branch would leave La Grande late in the afternoon three days a week and head to Joseph and then return as far as time permitted. After a rest, they would work their way back to La Grande, generally taking two days to work the line.

Sale of the Joseph Branch

In November 1993, Union Pacific leased and sold the Joseph Branch to the **Idaho Northern & Pacific** as a part of a package of rail lines in the area. To protect the part of the line with the greatest concentration of business, UP maintained the ownership of the right-of-way between La Grande and Elgin. The statement published by the Interstate Commerce Commission was that the Idaho Northern & Pacific would lease and operate the Joseph Branch from Milepost 0.0 at La Grande, to Milepost 21.0 at Elgin, and acquire by purchase the Joseph Branch from Milepost 21.0 at Elgin, to Milepost 83.58 at Joseph.

At first, the Idaho Northern & Pacific (INPR) operated regularly to Joseph, serving several sawmills along the line. However, these mills soon began to close, and freight service beyond Elgin became very rare. By March 1996, freight service to Joseph stopped. Abandonment of the line above Elgin was approved in April 1997. After several years of public debate, the Oregon Legislature earmarked $2 million for the purchase of the line and to start its rehabilitation. On March 31, 2002, the purchase of the line between Elgin and Joseph cleared escrow with an initial plan to reopen the line between Elgin and Wallowa. To operate the line, the Wallowa Union Railroad Authority was formed by and named for the two counties through which it passes. The organization assumed operation of the line on May 31, 2003. The first train back into Joseph finally operated during November 2003. The **Wallowa Union Railroad Authority** originally contracted with the Idaho Northern & Pacific to operate the line above Elgin as required by the on-line customers. However, beginning on December 19, 2003, Wallowa Union Railroad crews started doing the work. Excursion passenger service also began in 2003.

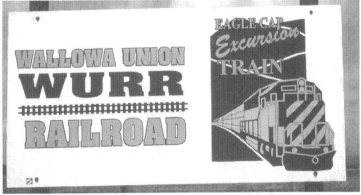

In 2004, this sign stood in Joseph, promoting the new freight and passenger rail service. Photo by Barton Jennings.

An issue for the excursion train was that Milepost 21.0 was north of Elgin in an inaccessible location. The Wallowa Union Railroad Authority wanted to operate out of downtown Elgin, reaching a new market for the passenger service. In the August 4, 2006, issue of the *Federal Register*, there was notice that the Wallowa Union Railroad Authority was going to "acquire from the Union Pacific Railroad Company (UP) approximately one half-mile of rail line between milepost 21.0 at Elgin, OR, and milepost 20.50 at the North line of Baltimore Street in Elgin, OR." This allowed the **Eagle Cap Excursion Train** to operate from that location. The first passenger train out of Elgin operated on November 18, 2006. First supporting, and now managing the passenger operations are the **Friends of the Joseph Branch**, a non-profit corporation. Unfortunately, about the same time, freight service on the line ended. Several additional efforts to use the railroad have been tried. Railbikes have also operated over parts of the line, typically around Joseph where excursion trains seldom operate.

The Eagle Cap Excursion Train passes through miles of scenic Northeast Oregon, like this area north of Elgin. Photo by Janet Dodson, courtesy of the Friends of the Joseph Branch.

Eagle Cap Excursion Train

The ***Eagle Cap Excursion Train*** is named after the Eagle Cap Wilderness Area in the Wallowa Mountains, which is the large series of mountains to the south and east of the Joseph Branch. The excursion train out of Elgin follows the Grande Ronde River downstream through rugged cliffs and timbered ridges, then up the wild and scenic Wallowa River. There is almost no time on the trip that the railroad is not almost in the shadows of this magnificent mountain country, which features glaciers, wild rivers, and elevations of near 10,000 feet.

"Go where cars can't take you!" is the way the rail ride is advertised, and it is certainly orrect as much of the route is far from public roads. A typical train ride will see more rafts and wildlife than cars and houses.

The loss of the railroad would have ended views like this one, located at the bridge over the Grande Ronde River near Rondowa. Photo by Barton Jennings.

In 2012, a modern depot was built at Elgin which features a gift shop, ticket office and historical railroad artifacts. It is open year-round for visitors, even when the train is not running. Information on the train schedules, depot hours and special events can be found on the website of Eagle Cap Train Rides.

The modern excursion train is now hosted in a modern Elgin station, built in 2012. Photo by Janet Dodson, courtesy of the Friends of the Joseph Branch.

Passenger Train Equipment

The passenger train equipment used on the Eagle Cap Excursion Train comes from across the country, and represents the mid-Twentieth Century era of railroading. The consist typically includes three passenger cars, plus a baggage car with a generator for electrical power.

Baggage Car #6741 is used as the power car for the consist. It was originally Southern Pacific #6741 and was built by Pacific Car & Foundry in 1962, and was known as an economy baggage-express car by many. This term comes from its boxcar-like construction, which lowered the cost to build the car. One end of the car includes an open-air viewing section for passengers.

Baggage car #6741 and the passenger car fleet parked next to the Joseph elevator. Photo by Barton Jennings.

Wallowa River – **Coach Car #3241** was originally built by Budd in 1938 as a parlor-observation car for the Santa Fe. In 1959, the car was rebuilt into 44-seat passenger coach #2948. It was sold to Penn Central (#2408) and then to New Jersey Transit as their #2408. The car lost its coach seats while owned by Bob McClanahan. It was refurbished by the Friends of the Joseph Branch in 2011 and now has table seating. Today, the stainless steel car carries the name *Wallowa River*.

Minam River – **Dining Car #1120**, which seats 64, was originally a 48-seat coach. It was built as Great Northern #1120 by Pullman Standard in 1947. The car was originally built for service on the *Empire Builder*, and then retrofitted in 1951 and moved to the *Western Star*. When retired, the car became New Jersey Transit #5309. It was rebuilt into a table car while being used behind Cotton Belt steam locomotive 819.

Grande Ronde River – Coach #2636 is a 56-seat coach. It was built as Illinois Central #2636 by Pullman Standard in 1947. The coach was one of four cars built to re-equip the *Green Diamond* passenger train, which operated between Chicago and St. Louis. At the time, it was given the name *Kankakee*. After the creation of Amtrak, the car was sold to the Black Hills Central in Hill City, South Dakota. All of the cars were later owned by Robert R. (Bob) Mc-Clanahan, former Cotton Belt/Southern Pacific Superintendent, who purchased the 1120 and 3241 in December of 1989, the 6741 in 1993 and the 2636 in 1997. These cars operated with the Cotton Belt 819 steamer, and were also leased to various tourist operators. The cars were sold to the Idaho Northern & Pacific Railroad in 1998 for use in Idaho. They were sold again and moved to the Joseph Branch operation in 2003. The cars have all received some level of refurbishment and their exteriors were painted in Fall 2014. The cars were subsequently named for area rivers.

Union Pacific used smaller Consolidation-type (2-8-0) steam locomotives on the branch until the 1950s when new diesels took over the line. Many of these were GP-7 locomotives, just as are operated today by the Wallowa Union Railroad Authority. **Locomotive #2083** was built in November 1953 as a GP-7 by the Electro-Motive Division of General Motors (EMD). It carries the construction serial number 18900. It was built for the Atchison Topeka & Santa Fe Railway as their #2883, which later rebuilt it to what they called a GP-7u and renumbered it #2083. **Locomotive #2085** has a very similar story. It was built in December 1952 as a GP-7 by EMD as Atchison Topeka & Santa Fe #2836. It was rebuilt as GP-7u #2085. It carries serial number 17647.

Wallowa Union Railroad Authority locomotive #2085 is shown at the new Elgin depot, powering an Eagle Cap Excursion Train. Photo by Janet Dodson, courtesy of the Friends of the Joseph Branch.

Locomotive #2087 is also a rebuilt Atchison, Topeka & Santa Fe locomotive. It started as #2839, an EMD GP-7 (built December 1952, serial number 17700). The Wallowa Union Railroad traded its two original GP-35 locomotives to Omnitrax for the three GP-7u locomotives, which had operated on the Central Kansas Railway.

WURR #4508 was a GP-35 locomotive, one of two initially owned by the railroad. They were later traded to Omnitrax for the current GP-7 locomotives. #4508 is shown at Wallowa on May 20, 2004. Photo by Barton Jennings.

The Wallowa Union Railroad also has two cabooses on its roster. **Caboose #25674** is one of one hundred Union Pacific class CA-9 cabooses built in July 1967 by International Car Co., of Kenton, Ohio. All were upgraded in 1973 so they could be used in pool service on any train systemwide. Caboose #25674 was one of the last five CA-9s in service on Union Pacific. It was donated and displayed at the Union County Fairgrounds in La Grande, before coming to the Wallowa Union Railroad Authority. The caboose has been refurbished and is in running order, and can be chartered with the full train for special occasions.

The Wallowa Union Railroad Authority also has a caboose that dates back to Great Northern caboose #X-378 in its collection. This is a 25-foot wooden caboose that was acquired and renumbered by the McCloud River Railroad in December 1939. **Caboose #025** was rebuilt first with sliding side doors, and then a new body after a wreck. After being used to move logging crews for a number of years, the caboose was again rebuilt, but with a body on only half the frame with an open area for a large toolbox. The caboose was retired in 1964 and sold to the Yreka Western Railroad as their #001, receiving the name *City of Yreka*. After that railroad closed down, it was moved to Elgin in June 2012, where it is now on display.

The newly-acquired passenger cars are shown next to the grain elevator at Joseph on May 21, 2004, the day before a passenger train chartered by the book's author. Photo by Barton Jennings.

The Joseph and Lake Wallowa area is a a popular entrance into the Eagle Cap Wilderness. Photo by Barton Jennings.

The Eagle Cap Wilderness

The Eagle Cap Wilderness area is Oregon's largest wilderness area, and features 359,991 acres. The area began in 1930 as a primitive area, and was then designated as wilderness in 1940. It became a part of the National Wilderness Preservation System with the passage of the Wilderness Act of 1964. As stated by the Wallowa–Whitman National Forest office, the "Eagle Cap Wilderness is characterized by high alpine lakes and meadows, bare granite peaks and ridges, and U-shaped glaciated valleys."

The wilderness area is surrounded by the Wallowa-Whitman National Forest and is located deep in the Wallowa Mountains, all in northeastern Oregon. The name Eagle Cap comes from what was once believed to be the highest peak in the mountains, Eagle Cap Peak at 9572 feet. The mountains used to be known as the Eagle Mountains before taking the name Wallowa Mountains, using the terms used by the Nez Percé, who hunted the region for bighorn sheep and deer, collected berries, and avoided the summer heat by spending the summer at higher elevations. They and other tribes started this practice by 1400 A.D., long before white settlers arrived about 1860.

The mountains are the major feature of the wilderness area. Sacajawea Peak is the highest at 9838 feet, and there are more than thirty peaks above 8000 feet in elevation. These upper slopes and peaks feature alpine timber and meadows. The higher elevations feature trees such as Engelmann spruce, larch, mountain hemlock, sub-alpine fir, and whitebark pine, while in the meadows can be found Indian paintbrush, larkspur, shooting star, and bluebells, providing very colorful summers. The highest lake in Oregon, Legore Lake at 8950 feet, is located here, as well as eight more at about 8000 feet. The Eagle Cap Wilderness does include some lower altitude valleys at elevations of approximately 3000 feet. Here, grasslands and ponderosa pine forest dominate, and the wilderness contains some small groves of old growth forest. Wildlife comes close to representing what was found here hundreds of years ago. This includes large animals like Rocky Mountain bighorn sheep and mountain goats, white-tailed and mule deer, elk, coyote, black bears, cougars, and even moose, grizzly bears, wolves and wolverines. Smaller animals such as badgers, marmots, pine martens, squirrels, pika, rabbit and other similar mammals exist. Lots of predatory birds, such as bald and golden eagles, peregrine falcons, and others are common. Trout are common in many of the lakes and streams, and the Oregon State record for golden trout was set here.

While motor vehicles are not allowed, there are more than 500 miles of trails in the Eagle Cap Wilderness. Summer sees hiking, backpacking and horseback riding, while winter includes backcountry skiing and snowshoeing. Hunting, fishing, camping and wildlife photography are common activities. A ride on the Eagle Cap Excursion Train is an introduction to this large and historic wilderness area.

La Grande to Joseph Route Guide

The route guide for the former Union Pacific Joseph Branch covers all of the stations and major features that existed between La Grande and Joseph, as well as many of the logging railroads that once connected to the line. The guide includes a history of the line and the locations that it passes through. It should be noted that this guide is not designed to be a complete history of the railroad, but instead it provides a great deal of information for those who like to ask, "Where are we and what once happened here?" Because of this, the guide includes information about current as well as former station locations, historic towns, and major stream crossings along the line.

Directions on this railroad will be based upon the railroad's own terminology. A train heading from La Grande to Joseph is heading east, so to the left is railroad-north, and to the right is railroad-south. To make matters easier, north and south directions will generally be used for the direction from the mainline, although the railroad certainly curves a great deal.

Throughout this guide, locations will be identified by mileposts. Railroads use mileposts, just like highways, to identify locations and to show the distances between them. The mileposts begin at La Grande, getting larger as the line heads to Joseph. The telegraph code for each station, as shown in the *Union Pacific System List of Officers, Agencies, Stations, Etc. No. 60*, dated January 1, 1930, is included with the station name.

Joseph Branch – La Grande to Elgin
Idaho Northern & Pacific

As stated elsewhere, Union Pacific still owns the Joseph Branch from La Grande (Milepost 0.0) to Elgin (Milepost 20.5). This trackage is leased and operated by the Idaho Northern & Pacific. The Idaho Northern & Pacific (INPR) acquired their lines in western Idaho and eastern Oregon from Union Pacific on November 15, 1993. The company is a subsidiary of Rio Grande Pacific Corporation (RGP). Rio Grande Pacific owns and operates four shortline railroads in six states (Idaho Northern & Pacific; Nebraska Central; New Orleans & Gulf Coast; Wichita, Tillman & Jackson) which haul more than 70,000 carloads of freight annually. They total more than 700 miles in length and serve approximately 140 freight customers. Each railroad provides badly needed rail service which saves and creates jobs for the local economy.

In Oregon, the INPR took over the **Joseph Branch** out of La Grande. This included leased track from MP 0.0 at La Grande, to MP 21.0 at Elgin; and purchase of the line from MP 21.0 at Elgin, to MP 83.58 at Joseph. The Idaho Northern & Pacific now operates La Grande to Elgin, and has sold the line from Elgin to Joseph to the Wallowa Union Railroad Authority.

The Idaho Northern & Pacific actually was created out of a number of lines in Oregon and Idaho. This included the **New Meadows Branch** in Idaho. This route included trackage rights on the New Meadows Branch between MP 0.00 and MP 1.0 at Weiser, Idaho; and on the Union Pacific mainline between MP 519.0 at Weiser, and MP 454.0 at Nampa, Idaho. The INPR also purchased the New Meadows Branch from MP 1.0 at Weiser, to MP 84.55 at Rubicon, Idaho. There was little business on the New Meadows Branch and the Interstate Commerce Commission approved its abandonment on November 1, 1995, and the last freight train operated on November 18, 1995. The rails were removed during the summer of 1996.

The Idaho Northern & Pacific was created to operate the Joseph Branch, and several other area lines, in 1993. Here, the company is switching the mill at Elgin a decade later. Photo by Barton Jennings.

The INPR also acquired the Payette and Idaho Northern Branches in Idaho through both purchase and lease. The routes **purchased** included (1) the Payette Branch from MP 0.39 at Payette, Idaho, to MP 27.0 at Emmett, Idaho; and (2) the Idaho Northern Branch from MP 28.0 at Emmett, to MP 99.68 at Cascade, Idaho. The INPR **leased** (1) the Payette Branch from MP 27.0 to MP 29.1 at Emmett; and (2) the Idaho Northern Branch from MP 5.0 at Maddens, Idaho, to MP 28.0 at Emmett. **Trackage rights** were obtained on the Idaho Northern Branch between MP 0.00 at Nampa, Idaho, and MP 5.00 at Maddens.

The Idaho Northern & Pacific operates the Joseph Branch out of a small facility at Island City, Oregon. Business along the line is primarily lumber, although several of these facilities have recently closed. Chemicals and some agricultural products are also moved over the railroad, as well as any freight interchanged with the Wallowa Union Railroad Authority.

0.0   LA GRANDE (RA) – The branch departs from La Grande at the mainline milepost 290.4 and at an elevation of 2788 feet above sea level. There is no wye at the junction. Instead, the Joseph Branch comes out of the east end of the La Grande Yard at Fir Street, and follows the two mainline tracks to the north. Near Island Avenue, Oregon Highway 82, the branch curves to the north and leaves town.

La Grande was a major terminal on the railroad, with miles of steep grades to the east and west. During the 1930s, La Grande was the home of the Second Division Superintendent for the Oregon-Washington Railroad & Navigation Company, and there was a full list of enginehouse, car shop, crew, and track maintenance supervisors and forces. The First Sub-Division went east to Huntington, Oregon, while the Second Sub-Division went west to Reith, Oregon.

To maintain the large number of steam locomotives necessary for the mainline and Joseph Branch, there were thirteen 85-foot, five 90-foot, and sixteen 110-foot stalls in the roundhouse, served by a 100-foot turntable. By 1950, the five 90-foot stalls were gone, but the rest remained in service. The foundations of the roundhouse can still be seen at the northeast end of the yard. There was also a 500-ton capacity timber coaling tower that had been built by the Snow Construction Company, as well as a 680-barrel oil tank with one oil column. There were four water columns scattered about the yard, supplied from a 65,000-gallon water tank and city water.

There was also a wye track, 10-pen stockyard with water and wagon chute for handling hogs, a 100-ton Fairbanks track scale, and a 610-ton capacity ice house. Standard clocks could be found in the dispatcher's office, telegraph office, and the enginemen's registration room. There were also section houses for the track gang that maintained the track from La Grande to Milepost 10.5. By 1948, the Joseph Branch was served by daily mixed trains #304 and #305. Train #304 would leave La Grande for Joseph at 7:00am, while #305 would return from a day's work at 5:00pm.

A Union Pacific freight heads east, departing LaGrande in May 2004. Photo by Barton Jennings.

The City of La Grande

The community of La Grande was originally to be called Brownsville, after Ben Brown, who settled here in 1861. A meeting of area residents was called to select the name and Brownsville was turned down. Instead, La Grande was chosen as a version of Grande Ronde Valley, reportedly suggested by Charles Dause, a young Frenchman living in the valley at the time. The first post office opened here on May 28, 1863, with Benjamin P. Patterson as postmaster and the operator of the first general store in the area. The City of La Grande was incorporated in 1865, and had a population of 13,082 at the 2010 census. Today, La Grande is the county seat of Union County.

La Grande was located on a part of the original Oregon Trail at the base of the climb over the Blue Mountains. Travelers headed to the west coast of Oregon had just finished a hard climb across the sagebrush covered mountains to the east and they were now confronted with the tree-covered, extremely steep and rugged Blues. The plentiful grass and water made the area a temporary camp for the many wagon trains coming through this area. With the initial settlement here, several settlers began to operate restaurants and inns for the many travelers passing through the area. Within a few years, several sawmills were working on making lumber from the surrounding trees. A grist mill and then a flour mill followed by 1865, and the Rynearsin brothers began manufacturing plows here, indicating an expanding agricultural effort in the valley.

The Oregon Railway & Navigation Company built through the flat area below town to the north in 1884, causing part of the town to move, creating "Old

Town" and "New Town" La Grande. Historically, La Grande was the base of the many helper locomotives and crews needed to push trains over the mountains to the east and west. Many trains were broken up or consolidated here, requiring a large railroad yard. A Pacific Fruit Express emergency icing station was located here until 1949. It was 1144 feet long and could handle 26 cars at a time. During the harvest season, it was also used to do initial icing, making sure that railroad refrigerator cars were cool to protect the fruit and vegetables harvested in the region.

While the roundhouse, icing platform, and many other related buildings and facilities are now gone, La Grande is still an important facility for Union Pacific. Many UP offices are located in the large, two-story brick station downtown at the end of Depot Street (the author's office used to be on the second floor on the east end). The rail yard is used to break up and consolidate trains fighting their way over the area mountains. Some crews are based here and mechanical inspections of some trains are still made. Rail traffic is very heavy with imports and exports moving through here on dozens of trains a day. La Grande is also a center for business in northeastern Oregon and the facilities here are designed to serve the local customers.

The large Union Pacific station still stands in downtown LaGrande. It once housed the management offices for the Joseph Branch. Photo by Barton Jennings.

The Timber Industry

When the railroad arrived at La Grande, the timber in the area became very valuable. La Grande became a center for the lumber business, especially after the construction of the Joseph Branch. George Palmer Lumber, Bowman-Hicks Lumber, Ponderosa Pine Logging, and others all had brokers here, and many had mills here too. One operator not already mentioned who had a sawmill in La Grande was Masters-Ewold Lumber Company. They served their mill with a Climax steam locomotive, a B23 class engine built in 1913. The steamer was sold off by 1922, about when the first timber shortages were being experienced and the mills were being consolidated into fewer owners. For those who don't know what a Climax steamer is, it is a geared locomotive, but one with the steam cylinders on each side of the boiler aimed

37

downward at about a 45 degree angle. This type of locomotive was much more rare than the Shay type.

The **George Palmer Lumber Company**, "Manufacturers of the Famous Looking Glass Pine," once had a major lumber facility at La Grande. It was located on the northwest side of town, where the Union County Fairgrounds now stands. This mill opened in 1907 and was built and run by the George Palmer Lumber Co., started by George Palmer, who was the company president. Palmer, who was born in Vermont and then moved to Iowa before coming to La Grande, was involved with several businesses here. The George Palmer Lumber Company was important to the Joseph Branch, as the company shipped a great deal of timber on the railroad from their holdings north of Elgin. When Palmer died in 1922, **Bowman-Hicks Lumber** acquired the mill and operated it until the early 1940s. The mill was removed, but the old office building survived, still being used today by the fairgrounds.

The second major lumber mill in La Grande was the **Mount Emily Lumber Company**. This mill was located along the Joseph Branch, just west of today's Interstate 84. A. J. Stange started the company by buying 100,000 acres of forest land through his Mt. Emily Timber Company. After several years back in Wisconsin working with his family, Strand returned to La Grande in 1920 and formed the Mount Emily Lumber Company. The large sawmill (a capacity of 50,000,000 board feet per year) began cutting wood on November 15, 1925. The same year, the company acquired the Grande Ronde Lumber Company and its rail operations.

The lumber company was a major operation for several more decades, running logging railroads throughout the surrounding mountains. However, as Strange got older, he sold the company to Valsetz Lumber Company in January, 1955. Valsetz renamed the company **Templeton Lumber Company**, temporarily shut down the mill and closed for good all of the logging railroad operations. In 1960, the lumber company was sold again, this time to **Boise Cascade**. Over the next several decades, Boise Cascade modernized the facility, added and subtracted product lines, and even built several related mills in the general area. However, by the late 1990s, things began to change and the industry was suffering in the area. In 2009, Boise Cascade announced that it would close its pine lumber mill in La Grande. A few plans to operate the mill resulted in some promise, and then in 2018, the mill was sold to Woodgrain Millwork.

The Sugar Industry

An interesting story related to the lumber industry at La Grande is that the Mount Emily Lumber Company built their mill near where the Oregon Sugar Company, a part of the Amalgamated Sugar Company of Utah, was built in 1898. This mill was incorporated by David Eccles, Charles W. Nibley, and George Stoddard to process sugar beets grown in the Grande Ronde Valley. After many local farmers refused to accept the low prices that the mill was offering, the Oregon Sugar Company tried to grow their own beets. However, they could not find sufficient land to buy. The mill didn't last long due to the shortage of sugar beets, and it was torn down in 1912 after several years of minimal operations.

The story of the sugar mill's founders may be even more interesting. David Eccles was Utah's first multimillionaire. He founded the Eccles Lumber Company, and built the Sumpter Valley and Mount Hood railroads. He married George Stoddard's daughter as his second wife (Eccles practiced the polygamy belief of his church). Records show that Stoddard was the local representative, with offices in both La Grande and Baker, Oregon. Charles Wilson Nibley was also a Utah millionaire, and also the fifth presiding bishop of The Church of Jesus Christ of Latter-day Saints. Nibley had managed several companies owned by the church, and was an acknowledged legal mind who used many tricks to claim land, including manipulating the Homestead Act and paying off investigating government agents. His writings also showed that he loved monopolies, believing competition was an "economic waste."

0.9   **INTERSTATE 84** – The railroad passes under Interstate 84, a 790-mile long highway from Portland, Oregon, eastward to Echo, Utah, east of Ogden. I-84 was once Interstate 80N, considered as a branch of Interstate 80. Built starting in the 1950s, it was renumbered in 1980.

Just north (railroad-east) of the Interstate is a spur track that serves the Ed Staub & Sons propane facility. Ed Staub & Sons was founded in Alturas, California, more than sixty years ago. It currently has branches in California, Oregon, Idaho, Nevada and Washington. The firm sells energy (propane, heating fuel, gasoline and diesel), fuel additives, and appliances.

Heading towards Elgin and Joseph, the railroad often closely follows Oregon Highway 82. Here, it is on the north side of the highway. The area north of here to Island City is the current growth area for the valley with several housing subdivisions, shopping

(Walmart), and small businesses being built out this way.

A Union Pacific switch job returns to LaGrande, and is shown passing through farmland just south of Island City, Oregon, in March 1986. Photo by Barton Jennings.

Union Pacific 2021 is parked north at LaGrande, waiting for an open track in the yard in 1986. Photo by Barton Jennings.

1.9   IDAHO NORTHERN & PACIFIC SHOPS – To the south are several tracks where the Idaho Northern & Pacific parks their locomotives and maintains their rail equipment. The railroad also has a small office here.

2.2   ISLAND CITY – Island City got its name because it was once located on an island. The island was formed by the Grande Ronde River and a slough which leaves the river west of town and rejoins it several miles to the east. The slough is south of the main river. When the railroad came through La Grande in 1884, the OR&N altered the course of the river to prevent the possibility of it flooding the train yards. At Island City, the water was drained off the slough but it has since washed out to become the current river channel.

The first settler in the Island City area was most likely Joseph Magrue, though Alexander Furgason settled here in 1862. The first commercial business was a grist mill built in 1872 by John Caviness and his partner, a Mr. Sterling. A post office opened here in 1873 with Sterling as the postmaster. Caviness and Sterling platted and dedicated the community in 1874.

Island City began to grow when Charles Goodnough opened a store and then organized the Island City Mercantile & Milling Company in 1884. The firm quickly became one of the largest businesses in Union County, operating a flour mill for many of the local farms and residents. The firm also had branches in several area towns, including Enterprise, Oregon. In 1896, the company had a capital stock of $75,000 and a surplus of $250,000. Its sales averaged $300,000 a year. By the late 1890s, the firm was sold off with the milling interest sold to the Pioneer Flour and Milling Company.

In 1948, Island City was a 7:10am flag stop for train #304. #305 passed through, again as a flagged train, at 4:40pm. In 1930, there was a freight platform here, as well as a two-pen stockyard. Today, the operator of the Joseph Branch (Idaho Northern & Pacific) has their base of operations on "E" Street here in Island City. A small agricultural co-op is also located here. The elevation is 2745 feet. Island City is basically a residential community supporting La Grande, and had a population of 989 in the 2010 census.

A general view of Island City in 1986. Photo by Barton Jennings.

2.5 GRANDE RONDE RIVER BRIDGE – Heading east toward Joseph, the railroad crosses Oregon Highway 82 and then the Grande Ronde River, putting the railroad on the south side of Highway 82. The river is pretty wide here and it takes two 80-foot through plate girder bridges to cross it. The railroad follows the Grande Ronde for quite some time, until it begins to follow the Wallowa River on to Joseph, Oregon.

The Grande Ronde River drains an area on the southeast side of the Blue Mountains, and the northwest side of the Wallowa Mountains. The river starts about twenty miles south of La Grande near the Anthony Lakes recreation area in the Wallowa-Whitman

National Forest. The river flows around the north side of La Grande, before entering about five miles of channel designed to provide irrigation water and to eliminate a winding marsh area. The river then turns north. In total the river is approximately 180 miles long and eventually flows into the Snake River.

The river received its name from French Canadian representatives of the Montreal-based fur trading firm, the North West Company. The name was common by 1820 and it means "Great Round" for the route that it took. The river supports populations of spring chinook salmon, summer steelhead, bull trout, mountain whitefish, and a number of other species.

3.3   **BAUM** – Baum is first two small spurs and then a 2000-foot siding, all to the south, to handle two major customers here. The chemical facility is operated by Hexion, while the second facility is a Woodgrain Millwork particle board plant. Both provide some nice revenue for the railroad. Going north, the line descends on a grade of about 0.3% and is at 2719 feet above sea level at Baum.

Hexion is a chemical company based in Columbus, Ohio. It produces thermoset resins and related technologies and specialty products. The company was created in 2005 by the merger of Borden Chemicals, Resolution Performance Products, and Resolution Specialty Materials, and the acquisition of Bakelite AG. The company was owned by two firms, which merged in 2010 to form Momentive Performance Materials Holdings LLC. The company was then renamed Hexion Inc. in 2015. Before 2005, this was a Borden Chemical facility. The railroad delivers tank cars and covered hoppers to this facility.

Woodgrain Millwork is a family-owned and operated company based in Fruitland, Idaho. The firm has manufactured wood doors, mouldings and windows since 1954. Woodgrain Millwork bought this particle board mill from Boise Cascade on November 2, 2018. Boxcars are generally used by the railroad to move the particle board.

4.6   PIERCE'S – This is a retired station that was also known as Pierce's Crossing for the highway-railroad grade crossing. Today, the grade crossing with Pierce Lane is at Milepost 4.2, just east of the west switch of Baum Siding. Pierce Road heads south past the La Grande airport to I-84 at Exit 268.

This was historically a small station used for agricultural loadings. There is some evidence that the station was named for Walter M. Pierce, the 17th governor of Oregon. Pierce lived in Eastern Oregon for a few years and developed a number of projects in the area, including farming and cattle, as well as the Hot Lake Sanatorium Company east of La Grande.

5.2   BOOTH'S LANE – This is another retired station. Booth Lane, located today at Milepost 4.9, is a road which runs straight to the east over toward Cove, a prosperous farming community at the base of Mount Fanny. Booth's was used to handle a great deal of business from this part of the valley. Immediately to the north of the tracks is Oregon Highway 82, which follows the railroad to and from Joseph.

5.6   CONLEY – Located at the Sandridge Road grade crossing, there was once a short siding to the north to serve several farm buildings. A small wooden elevator and an old crop storage barn built into an embankment still stand. After a steady 0.25% grade down from La Grande, the railroad starts a short stretch of 0.75% grade northward. The railroad continues to pass through open farmland.

While a flag stop for both trains #304 and #305, no time was provided in the timetable. Records from 1930 show that there was a freight platform here.

A. B. Conley, born in Tennessee and moved to the area in 1874 from Illinois, acquired a great deal of property in the area. He also served as Union County sheriff. The Conley family settled across the valley and were generally known as successful and prominent farmers. Some sources say that the station was named after J. Frank Conley, the son of A. B. Conley. Frank sold quite a bit of land to the Mormon Church so they could start the community of Nibley, so he may have been the one honored by this station name.

8.1   **ALICEL** – Alicel stands at the top of a small ridge at 2758 feet above sea level and about 50 feet above the surrounding area. The railroad was completed through Alicel in late 1890. The town was named by Charles Ladd for his wife, Alice, in 1890. When the railroad was being built to Elgin, locals planned a community in the middle of the valley that the railroad would pass through. Charles Ladd donated the land that the village grew on. On July 10, 1890, a station was established here which included a post office and store, operated by Dr. Cobb.

Three warehouses were built in 1896 to handle all of the freight from the area being shipped over the railroad. Within a short time, Alicel also boasted a school, two stores, a community church, blacksmith shop, a Farmers Union Hall, and a dance hall. A map from 1938 showed 38 blocks to the east. However, this was about the peak of Alicel's population, and the post office closed in 1972. Today, a PPG (Pendleton Grain Growers) elevator is the dominate feature here, with just a few houses. A railroad siding exists to the south. The former siding to the north is now gone. To handle switching when needed, the PPG elevator has its own car mover.

In 1948, Alicel was a 7:22am flag stop for train #304. Train #305 passed through, again as a flagged train, at 4:25pm. There was also a freight platform here during the 1930s. Heading north, the railroad begins a steady descent of about 0.5%. A number of farm complexes will be passed, but none rely upon rail service.

12.0 IMBLER (BR) – For those with allergies, Imbler can be problematic as it is the self-proclaimed "Grass Seed Capital of the United States." Among the producers here are Oregon Trail Seeds, Blue Mountain Seeds, and H. L. Wagner & Sons Seeds, although the town only has a population of about 300. Oregon Trail Seed was started by Curt and Annette Howell in May of 1993, using the warehouse of Jim Lindsey. They soon bought their own facility in North Powder, and then rented the building and bought the machinery at Grande Ronde Grain and Chemical, located in Imbler. The firm has since built their own seed conditioning and storage facilities at Imbler.

Blue Mountain Seeds produces more than 40 varieties of Kentucky bluegrass, plus other varieties as needed. The firm features dozens of bins holding from 80,000 to 100,000 pounds of seed each. New Jersey, New York and Illinois are big markets for the firm, where more than 75,000 acres of grass will be grown from the seed. The firm is based in Imbler and oper-

ates a number of facilities in the area. H. L. Wagner &
Sons Seeds has been operating for more than 80 years,
having been founded in 1935. The firm specializes in
grass seed. The firm's traditional warehouse is immediately to the south of the tracks at the east end of town.

The first town in the area was Summerville, platted on September 20, 1873, about four miles to the
northwest. Summerville was located on Ruckle Road,
the second road over the Blue Mountains. However,
when the railroad was built, Imbler quickly replaced
Summerville.

In the early 1890s, Jesse Imbler and his family
farmed land in this area, and a town was platted on
their farm. The Imbler post office was established in
1891 with Albert E. Imbler serving as the first postmaster. A depot was built the same year for the railroad. The Kerr Gifford Company elevator stands on
the site of the first flour mill here, built in 1903. In
1948, #304 stopped here at 7:32am and #305 at
4:15pm daily.

The railroad had a number of facilities at Imbler.
To handle the livestock business, the railroad had a
two-pen stockyard. There was also a freight platform
for general freight shipments. Imbler was also the
home of a track gang and their section houses. In 1930
when almost all track work was done by hand, the Imbler track gang maintained the track from Milepost
10.5 to 20.0.

The valley has begun to narrow here as the railroad heads northeast. Just to the east is Mount Harris
(5335 feet high, named for Joseph Harris, a pioneer
resident) while Mount Emily (6110 feet high) is to the
west. The story about how Mount Emily got its name
is worth a note here. There are two basic stories. The
first is that a family by the name of Leasy lived at the

foot of the mountain in pioneer days. The husband weighed about 100 pounds while the wife, Emily, weighed about 300 pounds. It is said that the husband named the peak after his wife because of her great size. The second story says that a very popular young lady by the name of Emily lived on the slopes of the mountain, and she was often visited by the young men of La Grande. It is obvious that the early settlers had a sense of humor, or at least those that passed on the stories.

13.0 TOMA – There is no sign today of this retired station. However, it was once located where the railroad and Highway 82 come back together northeast of Imbler. Little is known about the location except that it is at an elevation of 2714 feet and was apparently used as a construction camp when the railroad was being built.

14.5 WILLOW CREEK BRIDGE – Willow Creek is created by the merger of Fir Creek and Mill Creek a few miles to the west. The railroad crosses it on a 262-foot long, 18-span timber pile trestle, needed because Willow Creek merges with the Grande Ronde just to the east of the railroad. Just to the north of here, a culvert was installed in March 1986 to help handle flooding.

15.5 RHINEHART – Look for the grade crossing with Rinehart Lane, just east of where the Grande Ronde River comes briefly beside the railroad. The railroad and Highway 82 also start to take their own routes. Not far north of here was Rhinehart. This is a retired station that was never much more than a flag stop and freight platform on the Joseph Branch. While the railroad has always spelled the town with the first "h", the town was named for Henry Rinehart, a member of an early prominent family who settled the area.

Heading north, this is a view of the railroad as it enters the canyon near Rhinehart. Note the herd of deer at the base of the hillside. Photo by Barton Jennings.

East of here the railroad passes through a short curvy canyon, shared with the Grande Ronde River. Some of these curves are as sharp as ten degrees.

Union Pacific 2042 leads the Joseph local northwards alongside the Grande Ronde River towards Elgin on June 22, 1986. Photo by Barton Jennings.

16.3 RHINEHART BRIDGE – The bridge that crosses over the railroad and Grande Ronde River at this location was built in 1922 and is the original Oregon Highway 82 route. The bridge, from west to east, includes three skewed 40-foot reinforced concrete deck girder spans, a 140-foot steel nine panel Warren deck truss, and then two 30-foot deck girder spans. It also features a deck more than 19 feet wide, architectural railing and arched sidewalk brackets. The bridge and road are now closed to highway traffic.

The railroad and river curve sharply several times as they loop around the southeast end of Pumpkin Ridge, located to the northwest. To the east, invisible from the tracks, is Bennets Point.

The Union Pacific Joseph Local is heading north, viewed from the Rhinehart Bridge, in 1986. Photo by Barton Jennings.

During the 1980s, the Joseph Local still featured a caboose, as shown here at Rhinehart Bridge. Photo by Barton Jennings.

17.9 OREGON HIGHWAY 82 – Also called the Wallowa Lake Highway, the roadway between La Grande and Joseph passes overhead. Highway 82 is approximately 70 miles long and connects La Grande and Joseph. It is also part of the Hells Canyon Scenic Byway. The bridge and highway have recently been completely rebuilt.

From here, the railroad makes a series of gentle curves and then turns to the northeast to head into Elgin, Oregon.

20.1 PHILLIPS CREEK BRIDGE – This bridge is a three-span steel pile trestle bridge. In 2002, Phillips Creek was the subject of a report as part of the Grande Ronde Model Watershed Program. The report stated that Phillips Creek is a relatively small watershed containing about 33 square miles, or slightly over 24,000 acres. Phillips Creek empties into the Grande Ronde River in Elgin. Phillips and Little Phillips Creeks form to the northwest of Elgin, flow south, and then turn east around the south side of Elgin. They flow through timber-covered mountains, and are traditional steelhead spawning and rearing streams.

Immediately north of the Phillips Creek bridge, there is a long spur track to the west that is used to serve the Boise Cascade sawmill. This facility has for decades been a major source of freight business for the railroad, and a major source of local jobs. This mill explains why the Idaho Northern & Pacific/Union Pacific have kept the line between La Grande and Elgin while the Wallowa Union Railroad Authority has acquired the line from here to Joseph.

While Boise Cascade was not the first owner of the mill complex, Boise Cascade has operated the Elgin lumber mill since 1960. However, on May 16, 2018, Boise Cascade announced plans to curtail its lumber operation in Elgin, including sawmill, planer and shipping department. Under the change, the powerhouse, log utilization center, and Elgin Plywood Mill would remain operational.

In 1985, the remains of the old sawmill still stood in Elgin, a reminder of the past. Photo by Barton Jennings.

20.5 ELGIN (GN) – The traditional milepost for Elgin is 20.6, but with the sale of the line north of Milepost 20.5 to the Wallowa Union Railroad Authority, this milepost now makes more sense. Further details on Elgin can be found with the route description for the Wallowa Union Railroad Authority.

In 1912, a herd of elk was moved from Yellowstone to Joseph by train. A series of photos covered the move, many of which featured the stations along the Joseph Branch. Photo by William L. Finley from the William L. Finley Photographs Collection, circa 1900-1940, The Oregon Historical Society Library.

Joseph Branch – Elgin to Joseph
Wallowa Union Railroad Authority

As stated elsewhere, Union Pacific still owns the Joseph Branch from La Grande (Milepost 0.0) and Elgin (Milepost 20.5). However, east of here the railroad is now owned by the Wallowa Union Railroad Authority.

Elgin has always been a dividing point on the railroad. The track between La Grande and Elgin, built up the wide Grande Ronde Valley agricultural area, was built in 1890 by the Oregon Railway Extension Company. North and east of here, the railroad runs through narrow gorges and high-altitude pastures where timbering and livestock are the primary businesses. The railroad east of Elgin was built by the Oregon Railroad & Navigation Company in 1905-1908.

Elgin was also the dividing point for the operations of the Idaho Northern & Pacific (INPR) when it took over the line in 1993. The route from Milepost 21.0, just north of Elgin, southward to La Grande, remained the property of Union Pacific and was only leased by the INPR. East of that location, the line was sold to the INPR. The Wallowa Union Railroad authority acquired the INPR-owned line in 2003, and bought the track between Milepost 20.5 and 21.0 from Union Pacific in 2006 so they could operate their passenger excursion trains out of Elgin.

Idaho Northern & Pacific 2094 is being used to switch at Elgin in 2004. Today, this is the dividing line between the INPR and Wallowa Union Railroad. Photo by Barton Jennings.

20.5 ELGIN (GN) – Welcome to the "Jewel of the Blue Mountains." Indians originally called this area "Hunaha." Today, it is Indian Valley, which makes up the north end of the Grande Ronde Valley. This area was used by local tribes for hunting, fishing and collecting plants. In 1878, a bridge was built across the Grande Ronde here, attracting a lot of trade. It was for several generations a gathering place for trappers and hunters to replenish their supplies. Fort Baker, a blockhouse built here during the Indian Wars of 1878, also brought a great deal of attention to the location.

The community of Elgin was originally called Fishtrap because of the presence of Indian fishing gear found in the area. However, the town took the name Elgin when it received a post office on September 28, 1885, with W. B. Hamilton as the postmaster.

There are several stories about how Elgin received its name. The first is that W. B. Hamilton heard his niece and nephew (Lottie and Charlie) singing a ballad about the wreck of the steamer *Lady Elgin*. The *Lady Elgin* was loaded with a group called the Union

Guard, composed of Third Ward boys of Milwaukee, who formed an excursion to attend a mass meeting in the presidential campaign of 1860. The Union Guard went to Chicago to hear Stephen A. Douglas on September 7. On their way back to Milwaukee, sailing through a heavy fog on Lake Michigan, the ship was hit by the lumber schooner *Augusta*. The *Augusta* left the scene after being told that the *Lady Elgin* wasn't damaged. However, the ship then quickly sank with almost 300 people drowning. The song "Lost on the *Lady Elgin*" was a popular ballad written about the event.

Another story states that a manager and business investor from Elgin, Illinois, provided the name. This version is certainly not nearly as romantic as the first. It is also still denied by the Hamilton family.

By 1887, Elgin reportedly had several general stores, a livery, a hotel, and a church, as well as a nearby sawmill. The railroad reached here on October 25, 1890. Elgin was incorporated on February 18, 1891, and the town featured a pressure water system, electricity, 56 businesses and 18 sawmills. By 1908, there were reportedly 35 sawmills in the area, many using water power from the Grand Ronde River, as well as other area streams.

The extension of the line on to Joseph greatly hurt Elgin as much of the business came from communities further up the valley. Today, Elgin is actually a surprisingly small community, housing about 2000 residents. Among the finds here is the 1912 opera house which was designed as both an opera house and city government building. Praised for its acoustics and slanted seating arrangement, the opera house features plush draperies, box seats, an orchestra pit, elaborate backdrops, and decor in the rococo ("an elaborate style of architecture and decoration, imitating foliage, scrolls, etc.") style.

Elgin was the birthplace of Earl Avery Thompson, inventor of the manual transmission synchronizer. Thompson was born in Elgin, Oregon, on July 1, 1891. In 1923, he completed his work on the manual transmission synchronizer and became the leader of the team at General Motors Corporation that developed the first Hydramatic automatic transmission in 1940. His name was on nine of the fifteen patents involved.

Elgin and the Timber Industry

Elgin was on the edge of the timber in the mountains to the north, and this allowed it to develop quite a few lumber industries. Sawmills were built here as soon as settlers began to arrive, but most during the late 1800s were small and only served the local business needs. *An Illustrated History of Union and Wallowa Counties*, published by the Western Historical Publishing Company in 1902, has some detail about the early timber industry at Elgin. "Elgin is in close proximity to an extensive lumbering district lying to the north and west. There are eighteen sawmills tributary to the city as a supply and shipping point. The nearest is but two and a half miles distant from town while the farthest is twelve miles away. There are two planing mills kept in constant operation. One is owned by Spencer Brothers and the other by Sappington & Company. One of the sights at Elgin is the immense area just out of town on the northeast that is covered with stacks of lumber awaiting shipment."

In 1900, the wye track at Elgin was a busy place. Maps from the time show that it was lined with piles of railroad ties and cut timber, waiting to be shipped out over the railroad. At the time, the tail of the wye went several blocks west of Pine Street (today's 10th Avenue) to serve the H. D. Spencer & Co. planing mill and lumber yard. By 1911, Spencer was shown as manufacturing boxes, and he was also listed as the president of the Elgin Light & Power Company. H. D. Spencer & Co. was the only industry listed for Elgin in the 1911 *Wood-Using Industries of Oregon*, by the United States Forest Service. An interesting part of the study was that it was written by Howard B. Oakleaf. How is that for a name for someone working for the Forest Service? By 1913, the Hackett Lumber Company was also listed as being in Elgin.

In a report on the Elgin-Joseph Branch found in the October 1912 issue of *The Timberman*, a number of timber companies were reported on. It stated that a local timber yard reported that business was pretty fair. It also said that Harry Spencer, of the Elgin Box Factory, was involved exclusively in the box business, selling product locally and as far east as Colorado. It also stated that Hackett & Company was going to cut 1,500,000 feet that year, much of it cutting contract pine logs.

However, during the early 1900s, there was a large amount of consolidation in the lumber industry, allowing the construction of larger and more efficient sawmills to serve the national market. One of the first major mill operations at Elgin was the **Pondosa Pine Lumber Company**, often mistakenly shown as the Ponderosa Pine Lumber Company in newspapers. The company was founded by Wilber E. "Bill" Moore, who built his mills at Elgin to manufacture wood specialty products. Moore had other mills located just west of La Grande at Perry and east of La

Grande near Telocasset, served by Union Pacific off of their mainline.

According to the Forest Service of the United States Department of Agriculture, most of the lumber mills built in the Blue Mountains tended to produce four main products. The first was the better grades of lumber, which were cut and then shipped east where they would be remanufactured into new high-end products. The other three products typically served the local or regional markets: common lumber grades used locally for general construction, the poor lumber grades used to make fruit boxes, and the slab waste used to make lath, the thin flat strips of wood used as a plaster foundation or to support the tiles of a roof. The lath wood was also used to produce trellis or fence planks. However, Pondosa Pine produced higher value finished products such as window-shade rollers, ironing boards, wooden toys, boxes of all kinds, handles for kitchen utensils, and slats for window blinds.

As a part of this, Pondosa Pine worked as a planer mill doing custom work for other local mills. Its success allowed it to be rebuilt in 1931 after a severe fire, and the mill remanufactured approximately one million feet of lumber monthly, coming from several smaller mills at Elgin, as well as from company plants located at Wallowa and Joseph. A 1935 county map showed Pondosa Pine & Lumber Company on the west side of the track and south of Phillips Creek.

Bill Moore did more than just build several mills at Elgin (two existed during the early 1940s), he also built a baseball park which took the name Moore Field. The baseball field was completed in 1940 with a capacity of 3000, and was considered to be one of the best lighted fields in the Northwest. Before the end of World War II, ownership of the company transferred to the Ralph L. Smith Lumber Company of Kansas City, which continued to manufacture cut stock and mouldings at Elgin. Other area mills were bought, including the Mt. Joseph Pine mill which was acquired in November 1947. Ralph Smith sold his mills in 1960 and 1961 so he could retire.

Boise Cascade made their appearance in 1960 when they opened their Elgin lumber mill. The company created a number of different divisions here, making different products. However, on May 16, 2018, the company announced its intentions to close the sawmill, planer and shipping department. However, it was stated that the powerhouse and log utilization center would remain operational. The reasons cited for closing the mill included its age, size and technology,

The Railroad at Elgin

In 1948, #304 stopped here at 8:05am and #305 at 3:50pm daily. In 1985, UP had a section based here in the old station, using two motorcars to work on the track. On March 5, 1986, this book's author received a phone call that the Joseph Local had hit the Elgin motorcar at Milepost 21.35. Apparently, some local vandals were trying to see what would happen when a train hit a motorcar. The motorcar had been chained down (the chain was cut) and a police investigation determined that two people wearing tennis shoes had cut the chain and sent the motorcar down the track. At one time, Elgin had a Union Pacific caboose on display. It was later burned almost beyond recognition and moved to a local scrap yard. Be on the lookout for two people wearing tennis shoes and carrying a large bolt cutter, or someone with a pocket full of matches!

The Elgin depot is shown in December 1985, used by the local section gang. Photo by Barton Jennings.

This is a view of the back of the Elgin depot in 1985. Note how a set of tracks ran around the east side of the station. Photo by Barton Jennings.

For years, there have been a siding and a wye to the north of the mainline between Baltimore and Detroit Streets. Just south of Baltimore Street is a Pendleton Grain Growers elevator to the north, with the Elgin Opera House to the south. Several more grain elevators once lined the tracks to the east.

During the 1930s, there was a 4-pen stockyard here, plus the typical freight platform. For the steam locomotives, there was a 48,000 gallon water tank which was supplied from city water. Finally, there were section houses here for a track gang that maintained the track from Elgin eastward to Milepost 28.75.

Eagle Cap Excursion Train

The Eagle Cap Excursion Train operates trips over the railroad north of Elgin. Passenger service originally began in 2003, operating out of the end of the line at Joseph, and from other communities along the line. This was due to the property line between the Wallowa Union Railroad Authority and Union Pacific/Idaho Northern & Pacific being at Milepost 21.0. After an agreement was made that let the passenger train serve Elgin, most trips now originate here. A new depot was built in 2012 to house the operations. Located at 300 Depot Street, the building contains a gift shop, ticket office and historical railroad artifacts and is open to visitors year-round.

The Friends of the Joseph Branch is a volunteer organization that supports the railroad and manages the passenger train. Members work as volunteers on the train, including engineers and trainmen, conductors, and car hosts. The organization also assists with long-term planning to ensure the continuation of the passenger rail service on the Joseph Branch line.

The Eagle Cap Excursion Train operates out of this modern station, located in Elgin. Photo by Ed Spaulding, courtesy of the Friends of the Joseph Branch.

21.0 YARD LIMIT – After Union Pacific sold the line, this was the dividing line between Wallowa Union Railroad Authority and Idaho Northern & Pacific/Union Pacific ownership. Under Union Pacific, this was the north yard limit, the location where trains had to start operating prepared to stop for another train. This was due to the number of industries that needed rail service in Elgin.

On September 29, 2006, the Wallowa Union Railroad Authority acquired a half-mile of track from here into downtown Elgin to allow it to operate out of that community. The purchase also included land adjacent to the tracks that created room for a station, boarding area, and parking. The railroad ran its first train out of Elgin on November 18, 2006.

Heading east toward Joseph, the railroad closely follows the Grande Ronde River through near-wilderness. Over the next twenty-six miles, the railroad has only one public grade crossing.

This photo shows carloads of lumber coming off the Joseph Branch in 1986. The train is deep in the Grande Ronde River gorge. Photo by Barton Jennings.

22.7 GORDON CREEK BRIDGE – William Gordon, a rancher, had a place on this stream in the early 1870s and it bears his name. Gordon Creek starts at Gant Springs, about six miles to the northwest, and flows into the Grande Ronde River just to the south (compass-east). The railroad crosses it on a three-span timber pile trestle.

Heading east, that is Bolly Bluff across the river to the east (railroad-south). As the river and railroad squeeze between hills, trains pass Andys Rapids. This is probably the only large set of rapids on the river between Elgin and Palmer Junction.

24.9 GULLING – To the north is a 1650-foot-long siding at 2604 feet above sea level. Gulling was a flag stop for trains #304/#305 in 1948 and was often used to hold trains while another switched the businesses in Elgin.

Eastbound, the train passed through at 8:15am. Westbound, it came through at 3:37pm.

Gulling is deep in the Grande Ronde gorge, with tall hills on both sides of the river.

In 2004, the Gulling station sign still stood alongside the track, shown here as an excursion train stops at the location. Photo by Barton Jennings.

A Union Pacific work train is shoving north at Gulling with some track materials in 1986. Photo by Barton Jennings.

26.5 PARTRIDGE CREEK BRIDGE – This is a single span timber pile trestle. Partridge Creek is a small stream that flows off the hillside to the north. It forms a wide enough valley that a jeep trail also uses the grade from Palmer Junction Road on the top of the mountain down to near the tracks.

On May 6, 1986, nine freight cars (two chip cars and seven box cars) derailed from the La Grande-bound local (using UP 2000, 2031) at Milepost 25.75, just west of here. To quote the derailment investigation notes: "climbed east end of bridge, rode rail 20 feet, fell off west end 26.51 bridge (due to track warp), fell north." The result of this derailment was 0.69 miles of rebuilt track. Everything had to be brought in by train or hirail, and there was almost no shoulder to work with. West of here at Milepost 26.0, trains pass over the sharpest curve on the line at sixteen degrees. To find it, listen for the wheel-to-rail singing.

This is a photo of the May 6, 1986, derailment just west of Partridge Creek Bridge. Note that the train had boxcars full of lumber, and cars of wood chips. Photo by Barton Jennings.

30.1 MILL CREEK BRIDGE – The railroad crosses Mill Creek on a one-span timber pile trestle. There are a large number of Mill Creeks in Oregon, most being traced back to the presence of sawmills on them.

30.5 CABIN CREEK BRIDGE – Draining an area toward Nine-Mile Ridge to the west (railroad-north), it takes three deck plate girders (two 20-footers and one 25-footer) to cross Cabin Creek.

30.9 CABIN CREEK – The station, now retired, is at about 2460 feet of elevation. The station was named for the nearby stream named Cabin Creek.

The area to the east of here is known as Rysdam Canyon. According to several sources, Rysdam Canyon is a valley that is located southwest of Duncan Canyon, east of Moon Canyon and west of Howard Butte. Rysdam Canyon has an elevation of 2418 feet.

32.5 YARRINGTON ROAD – This is the first public grade crossing since Elgin, twelve miles to the west. It will be fourteen miles to the east before the railroad sees its next public road grade crossing. Yarrington Road begins at Oregon Highway 82 about a mile east of Elgin, and heads north to here, providing access to several ranches.

Immediately to the south, Yarrington Road bridges over the Grande Ronde River using a bridge that was built in 1906, but not installed here until 1925. The bridge includes a 150-foot-long main through truss span on the south end, and a smaller 100-foot through truss on the north end. Known as the Yarrington Road Bridge, or the Palmer Junction Bridge, it was built by the Lackawanna Bridge Company of

Buffalo, New York, and installed by P. S. Easterday & Company of Walla Walla, Washington.

32.6 SCHOTTE CREEK BRIDGE – A. C. Schotte owned land in the area that he sold to the George Palmer Lumber Company. The railroad crosses the stream using a three-span timber pile trestle. During steam days, there was a water tank here. Today, the stream is known as Moses Creek on many maps.

32.9 PALMER JUNCTION – Palmer Junction was once a very busy location on the railroad, being a junction with the logging railroad of the George Palmer Lumber Company, and later the Grande Ronde Lumber Company. With the construction of a logging railroad up Lookingglass Creek, a post office opened here on April 17, 1909, the same year that the Looking Glass Store was opened by Palmer Lumber. The Palmer Junction School also was open for a number of years to the west up Moses Creek. However, logging in the area by Palmer ended in the 1920s and the post office closed on July 17, 1937.

The May 27, 1911, issue of the *American Lumberman* had a significant report on the George Palmer Lumber Company. It stated the following.

> *"This is where the famous "Looking Glass Pine" is manufactured. This product, the name of which has come to denote quality, takes its name from Looking Glass creek, a mountain stream flowing through the company's timber holdings, thirty-five miles north of La Grande, on the Elgin branch of the Oregon & Washington Railroad & Navigation railroad. Here, at Palmer Junc-*

tion, the company's logging road connects and runs out into the timber with twenty miles of main line and numerous branches. A glance at the equipment of these camps will show the extent of the operations. This equipment consists of one 70- and one 45-ton Shay locomotive, two 4-line Clyde steam skidders, two McGiffert steam loaders, four donkey engines, machine shop, blacksmith shops, pumping station, water tank cars for supplying water to machines and fighting fires, thirty head of horses, and fifty 41 foot steel log cars equipped with stakes and Eau Claire safety trip pockets."

The October 1912 issue of *The Timberman* also had a report on what they called the Elgin-Joseph Branch. It included a great deal of information about Palmer Junction.

"At this point the Geo. Palmer Lumber Co.'s logging road connects with the Elgin branch. Standard steel flats and an 80-ton Shay bring the loads from the woods to the Junction, where they are transported to La Grande, a distance of 33 miles, while another Shay assembles the loads. Four Willamettes and a Washington Iron Works donkey, two Clyde Iron Works skidders and two Clyde loaders constitute the steam equipment, in addition to the teams. At the present time over 150,000 feet is going out daily. The company just completed new portable camps at Looking Glass; one building is 64 feet and the other 96 feet, each 16

feet wide. These camps are built in multi-
ples of 16 feet and can be quickly placed
on cars. The company say they find the steel
logging flat the most serviceable car they
have yet been able to use in the woods. They
are practically unbreakable and carry very
heavy loads The company are just opening
up a new camp at Looking Glass, which
will be known as Camp No. 4. A dam will
be thrown across the Looking Glass and the
logs loaded on the cars with a Clyde loader."

Another article in *The Timberman* (March 1915) provided more information about the railroad and its operations. This article stated that much of the logging was on hillsides 600 feet above the logging railroad. At first, the timber contractor used an ordinary two-log chute which was 1600 feet long and had a drop of approximately 600 feet. However, many of the logs were destroyed at the bottom of the chute due to the speed that they obtained. To better control the logs, the contractor "mounted a donkey drum at the upper end of the chute, also a 6 hp gasoline engine, which was connected to drum shaft by an 8 inch belt engine and shaft running continually. When letting down a string of logs one man applies the brakes. When the run of logs is released near the bottom of the grade, he releases the brakes and applies the friction to pull the cable and holdback block up for the next trip."

George Palmer Lumber Company Locomotives

The George Palmer Lumber Company reportedly had at least four Shay locomotives. Palmer Lumber #1 was a B45-2 Shay (construction number 1894) built

March 1907 for the company. A B45-2 Shay means that it weighs 45 tons and has two trucks and three cylinders. Shay #1 was assigned mostly on the logging lines. After Bowman-Hicks acquired the company in 1923, it was based at Maxville to move logs off of the many logging spurs in the hills. It was for sale in 1934 following the closure of the Maxville operation and eventually scrapped.

Palmer Lumber #2 was a C70-3 Shay (cn 2144) built March 1909 for the company as a wood burner and was assigned to Palmer Junction. The C70 class means that the Shay has three trucks, three cylinders, and weighs 70 tons. It became Bowman-Hicks #2 and was assigned to Wallowa and rebuilt as a coal burner. It was sold to Kosmos Logging in Washington and was eventually scrapped.

Palmer Lumber #3 was the biggest yet, being a C100-3 Shay (cn 2845) built November 1916 as an oil burner for the company. It also worked at Bowman-Hicks #3 before being sold in 1937 to Kosmos Logging in Washington. It was scrapped. This 100 ton locomotive is actually a relatively famous locomotive in Shay history as it was the first one built with a super heater.

Palmer Lumber #4 was originally built in August 1918 for the U.S. Spruce Production Company, established by the U.S. Army to provide spruce timbers for airplane construction during World War I. However, this oil burning C70-3 Shay (cn 3008) was almost immediately sold to Palmer Logging. Bowman-Hicks also operated it as #4 and finally sold it to the Alaska Junk Company in Portland in 1939 where it was scrapped.

Grande Ronde Lumber Company

The George Palmer Lumber Company was not the only firm that logged around Palmer Junction. An interesting legal note about Palmer Junction is found in the 1921 *Poor's Manual of Railroads*. It states that the Oregon-Washington Railroad & Navigation Company had leased 3.63 miles of trackage rights to the Grande Ronde Lumber Company near Palmer Junction.

A May 1, 1920, National Forest timber sale report covered the subject, and reported on a request from the Grande Ronde Lumber Company to expand their timber rights to cover the last of the timber that could be reached by their logging railroad. While the report goes into great detail about the timber and what they felt could economically be logged, the report also provides a great deal of information about the railroad operations of the Grande Ronde Lumber Company.

First, some background on the lumber company would be appropriate. The Grande Ronde Lumber Company was based in Perry, Oregon, about four miles west of La Grande on the Union Pacific mainline. It started building a sawmill there in 1890. According to the October 1912 issue of *The Timberman*, the firm operated a sawmill, planing mill and box factory. The article stated that "The company operate twelve miles of logging railroad, using Heisler and Shay locomotives. The Shay operates on the road and the Heisler switches and assembles the loads."

The railroad followed the upper end of the Grande Ronde River until it reached the timber holdings of the Mount Emily Lumber Company. In 1925 Mount Emily Lumber purchased the Grande Ronde Lumber Company logging railroad as the Grande Ronde

Lumber Company was closing its mill and moving to Pondosa, Oregon. Over the years, to supplement the timber west of La Grande, timber was acquired both east of La Grande and along the Joseph Branch.

The National Forest report stated that the timber was "on the watershed of Looking-glass Creek, a tributary of the Grand Ronde River, the confluence of which is at Palmer Junction, a station on the Joseph branch of the O. W. R. & N. Company. The Grande Ronde Lumber Company has been logging on the Looking-glass watershed for the past three years and now has its railroad grade up to the Forest boundary." The report further described the railroad by stating that it extended ten miles "from the Joseph branch of the O. W. R. & N. Company up Looking-glass Creek to the Forest boundary." The report also stated that "The Grande Ronde Lumber Company is logging their adjacent timber chiefly with horses, rolling the logs down the steep pitches."

This logging railroad went up Lookingglass Creek to the junction with Little Lookingglass Creek. There, the railroad turned west to follow the main branch of the stream. At the time of the request, the railroad ended at the edge of the National Forest, where Eagle Creek flows in from the southwest. The request to buy this additional timber seemed urgent as the lumber company planned to soon remove the logging railroad and use it on the company's new road above Hilgard, west of La Grande.

The Grande Ronde Lumber Company actually operated a second logging railroad here, across the river and a bit to the east up Duncan Creek. This line was built in 1919 and included a bridge across the Grande Ronde River that washed out from high waters during

Spring 1920. This logging was to be finished by Spring 1921 and the railroad removed.

According to several sources, the Grande Ronde Lumber Company operated with four steam locomotives; three Heisler and one Shay. The Heisler steam locomotive was one of three basic designs of geared logging engines. It was invented and patented in 1892 by Charles L. Heisler, an engineer at the Dunkirk Engineering Company, located in Dunkirk, New York. Heisler steam locomotives were unique in that they featured two cylinders at a downward, 45-degree angle on each side of the boiler where they drove a center drive-shaft that drove each axle. The locomotives were built by the Stearns Manufacturing Company.

The oldest of the three Heislers was #105, a two-truck locomotive built in June 1906 (cn 1091). It later was sold to the Meacham Lumber Company. Locomotive #104 was another two-truck locomotive, and was built in January 1924 (cn 1496). It later became Stoddard Lumber Co. #104. The newest and largest of the Heisler locomotives was #5, a three-truck locomotive built in March 1924 (cn 1501). It was originally built for the Ostrander Railroad Company, and later became Big Creek & Telocaset #5.

The fourth locomotive was a two-truck Shay #103, built in November 1909 (cn 2241). It later became Stoddard Lumber Co. #103. The Shay locomotive was the most widely used geared steam locomotive, being designed by Ephraim Shay about 1877. Built by Lima Locomotive Works, a Shay had two or three cylinders mounted vertically on the engineer side of the locomotive. The cylinders powered a drive shaft that connected to all of the wheels on the locomotive.

33.1 LOOKING GLASS CREEK BRIDGE – Union Pacific spelled this name as two words, but most maps show the creek as one word: Lookingglass. The creek bears the name of Lookingglass, a chief of the Nez Percé, who was so called by the whites because he carried with him a small looking-glass. His Indian name was "Apash-wa-hay-ikt." Lookingglass was one of the Nez Percé chiefs who joined Chief Joseph on his march toward Canada in 1877.

This stream drains the Blue Mountains to the northwest of Palmer Junction. During the winter, an active ski resort (Spout Springs) keeps the area busy up at Tollgate at the headwaters of the creek. Unlike most creeks on this line, the railroad requires two 40-foot deck plate girder bridges, the result of one too many washouts. Old photos from the United States Department of Agriculture, Forest Service, collection show that in 1913 this bridge was a timber pony truss bridge.

About two miles up Lookingglass Creek is the Lookingglass Fish Hatchery, located where Palmer Lumber once had their Logging Camp Number One. The hatchery was constructed in 1982 as part of the Lower Snake River Compensation Program, a program designed to make up for the loss of spring Chinook and summer steelhead caused by four federal dams constructed on the lower Snake River. This hatchery primarily produces spring Chinook for the Grande Ronde and Imnaha rivers. The hatchery actually functions "as an adult collection, egg incubation, and rearing and release site for the spring Chinook destined for the Grande Ronde River systems."

33.7 LOOKING GLASS – This community is named for the nearby creek with the same name. A few scattered houses still exist here, plus a number of foundations. The line will soon begin a long, hard climb eastward toward Joseph. The community is at an elevation of 2377 feet in elevation, while Joseph is at 4142 feet.

In 1948, Looking Glass was an 8:37am flag stop for train #304. #305 passed through, again stopping only when flagged, at 3:15pm. In 1985, two motor-cars were kept here to give section crews access to the canyon. Just east of Looking Glass between Mileposts 34 and 35, the hillsides alongside the railroad were known as a slide area and crews were kept busy digging out the ditches and keeping the track clean during the wetter periods of the year.

At one time, a 40-car-long siding existed to the north. By the 1980s, it was a 2080-foot-long spur with the switch at the west end. The grade can clear-ly be seen to the north. Several roads reach into this community, including Lookingglass Road which fol-lows the creek, Moses Creek Lane from the west, and Lookout Mountain Road which climbs the mountain-side to the north. Just railroad-east (compass-north) is a popular river access point. Further east, the railroad is squeezed in between the river to the south and a large hillside to the north. Note the drier hillside to the north, which is exposed to the sun most of the day, has less vegetation than the hillside across the river to the south, which is generally shaded.

In 1930, the railroad had a number of facilities here. There were section houses for the track gang that maintained the track from Milepost 28.75 to Mile-post 37.0. A 48,000 gallon water tank was here for the steam locomotives. There was also a 3-pen stockyard and a freight platform here.

While there were once a number of railroad facilities at Looking Glass, today the railroad mainly passes by scenic streams and mountains. Photo by Barton Jennings.

36.7 UNION-WALLOWA COUNTY LINE – Traveling towards Joseph, the railroad makes a turn of more than 126 degrees using a 10-degree curve to change the direction of travel from heading northeast to heading south. This is the farthest north that this line goes. The railroad will cross the county line five times in the next seven miles.

Union County, to the west, has its seat in La Grande (after several moves back and forth between La Grande and Union). The county was split from Baker County on October 14, 1864, and was named due to the support of area residents toward maintaining the United States during the Civil War. The county has the Blue Mountains to the west and the Wallowas to the east, basically covering the Grande Ronde Valley. The population of the county is more than 25,000, and the Forest Service reportedly owns almost half of the land in the county.

Heading east, the name Wallowa will be discussed many times with the Wallowa Mountains, Wallowa River, and the town of Wallowa. Here, **Wallowa County** will be explained. It was created on February 11, 1887, out of the eastern portion of Union County. The line between the two counties was changed in 1890, 1900, and 1915, making it sometimes difficult to use old historic maps of the region. Wallowa County's population in 2010 was 7008, making it Oregon's fourth-least populous county. Enterprise serves as Wallowa's county seat.

There is some question about the source and meaning of the name Wallowa. Some sources state that it is a version of a Nez Percé term for a structure of stakes (a weir) used in fishing. Other sources say that it is a Nez Percé word for "winding water." The Lewis and Clark Expedition noted the river and used the name Wil-le-wah.

36.9 GRANDE RONDE RIVER BRIDGE – This is the lowest point on the line at 2313 feet (okay, the areas just off each end of the bridge are a bit lower – 2309 feet to the east and 2307 feet to the west). The bridge is made up of four 60-foot deck plate girder spans.

West of here, the railroad has been following the Grande Ronde River. East of here, it follows the Wallowa River to Joseph. The Grande Ronde continues north and then turns east to flow into the Snake River. North of here, the river is federally protected for 43.8 miles to the Oregon-Washington border.

A passenger train poses on the Grande Ronde River Bridge in 2004, part of a special charter event. The photographers soon got wet – note the rain coming over the mountain. Photo by Barton Jennings.

The Grande Ronde River is a nationally renowned sport fishery, reportedly one of the top three in the region. Wild and hatchery stock of spring Chinook, fall Chinook, summer steelhead and rainbow trout are popular. The river also supports a wide variety of wildlife, including bighorn sheep, elk, mule and whitetail deer, black bears, cougars and mountain goats. It is also a wintering area for bald eagles.

The river has seen a steady increase in recreational use, including fishing, floating (rafting, canoeing and kayaking for overnight use), and big game viewing and hunting. As can be seen from the train, the route also features tremendous views of the Blue Mountains and typical western landscapes. Forests, native bunchgrass slopes, narrow valleys created by seasonal streams, and other views change almost by the minute.

A Wallowa Union passenger train pauses on the Grande Ronde River Bridge, part of the recreational use of the area. Photo by Ed Spaulding, courtesy of Friends of the Joseph Branch.

37.5   RONDOWA – There was once a short 7-car spur track here, with a small freight platform. The location was so small that it wasn't even a flag stop for the railroad. However, there was a post office at Rondowa 1909-1915. The name Rondowa was made up by taking the names of the two rivers which join here, the Grande Ronde and the Wallowa. Some sources state that it was created by railroad officials, others say that it was created by John Anthony, who operated a hotel and restaurant here. There was a post office here from June 1909 until October 1915. While there are several dirt roads to Rondowa, they are generally closed during late summer and fall.

39.3   KIMMELL – During the 1980s, Kimmell was the dividing point between the two track sections that worked on the branch. Kimmell is a rare siding (3940 feet long) in the canyon, providing a place for trains and equipment to pass. The siding is located to the north along the hillside.

There was never a town, store or post office at Kimmell. The elevation here is at 2354 feet and the railroad is climbing at 0.5% as it heads east.

40.1 WALLOWA-UNION COUNTY LINE – This is another crossing of the county line, this time caused by the rail line curving back and forth while the county line makes a short turn to the east, a kind of stair-step line running north to south, trying to follow the major ridge line in the area. Heading toward Joseph, the railroad passes from Wallowa County back into Union County.

40.3 HOWARD CREEK BRIDGE – Look for the six-span timber pile trestle. To the north is Howard Meadows, up on Howard Butte, the source of Howard Creek. The road up there is Brown Road (three out of four isn't too bad). The name Howard comes from Abe Howard who took up a homestead in the Howard Meadow area in 1885. Howard was killed when a horse fell on him, and his sons buried him on the north edge of the meadows named for him.

In 1910, the George Palmer Lumber Company hired Morrison-Knudsen to construct a logging railroad off the main line up Howard Creek for a distance of five miles to a logging camp called Camp Five. The last three miles climbed a 6% grade and required some heavy earthwork. This railroad opened up the Grossman country for timber harvest. The line was operated out of what was known as Camp 5, a location still shown on some maps at the upper end of the narrow Howard Creek Canyon. A number of spur lines were built up various creek beds and over mountain tops, with small Shay locomotives used on the spur tracks and the larger Shays handling the moves to the Union Pacific Joseph Branch.

In 1922, the Bowman-Hicks Lumber Company purchased the Palmer Lumber Company operation and their Camp 5. Bowman-Hicks felt that there was enough timber to build a more permanent logging base in the area of Camp 5. The plan was for a full town that could house approximately 500 people, and there would need to be water and level ground for the railroad. By this time, the railroad had crossed Akers Butte and reached Bishop Creek. The area east of Akers Butte included the large Bishop Meadows, a site that met the needs of the lumber company.

In 1923, construction of a logging camp began with new tracks being used to hold camp cars, while some workers lived in tents. By summer, Camp 5 was closed and the new logging town of Maxville was in business. The name Maxville came from the company's superintendent, J. D. McMillan. The community became known as Mac's Village, or Maxville. The post office moved to here from Camp 5, and by fall the town included a school, a bunk house, a mess hall, baseball field, a swimming hole, and a doctor's office. The logging business surpassed the original plans with almost 800 single workers having to be housed, plus housing for the many married workers and managers. A unique feature was that running water was available throughout town.

Another unique part of the town was that many workers had been brought in from several operations in the Deep South. This meant that 50 to 60 of its citizens were African-American. Its black residents lived in a group of portable houses across the tracks from the white residents. There were also separate schools for white and black students, unique for Oregon. A year later, Bowman-Hicks purchased the Nibley-Mimnaugh Mill in Wallowa. To connect the mill to the timber, sixteen miles of track was built from the Maxville area to Wallowa. The combined locomotive fleets were kept busy hauling timber to Wallowa and to the Union Pacific line for movement to other mills.

The Depression of 1929 hit Bowman-Hicks hard. Track was quickly removed where it wasn't needed and roads were built, allowing trucks to bring the timber to the mills. Maxville was officially closed in 1933, and a few of its buildings were saved and moved to Wallowa. The post office also closed in 1933, and the last of the tracks were retired. However, the land remained with the timber company for some time, and a 1935 map shows the property along the general route as still belonging to Bowman-Hicks Lumber Company. The only things that can be found at Maxville today are a pond, a large log house, and several roads. Also, the grade up Howard Creek has been widened and leveled for use by modern day vehicles.

40.6 VINCENT – Vincent was the railroad station that officially connected with the Palmer Lumber railroad up Howard Creek. The spot chosen was a rare wide spot along the river. For years there were several tracks here, then just a spur track, but now all of the tracks are gone. A post office was also here for a short period of time (1914-1923), but reports have it several miles up the logging railroad, probably at Camp Five. Vincent was reportedly named for Vincent Palmer of the Palmer Lumber Company. There is some indication that the Palmer Lumber Company ran their trains over the branch for several years to connect various logging lines to their mill.

In 1948, Vincent was an 8:54am flag stop for train #304. Train #305 passed through, again as a flagged train, at 2:58pm. There were once section houses here for a track gang (Mileposts 37.00-45.25) as well as a freight platform.

The Wallowa River wanders between Union and Wallowa counties in this area, forming a crooked but scenic railroad route. Photo by Barton Jennings.

41.1 UNION-WALLOWA COUNTY LINE – The county line is running north-south here, while the railroad runs northwest to southeast. The railroad passes from Union County and back into Wallowa County when heading east towards Joseph.

42.3 FISHER CREEK BRIDGE – This is a small creek which tends to run dry during late summer. It only takes a single-span timber pile trestle to cross it. However, note that the stream can move a great deal of material, based upon the alluvial fan in the Wallowa

River. An alluvial fan is a deposit of debris where a stream flows into a larger body of water.

42.6 WALLOWA-UNION COUNTY LINE – The railroad again crosses the county line, heading back into Union County. The county line has again turned east-west while the rail line keeps running northwest to southeast.

43.5 UNION-WALLOWA COUNTY LINE – The county line has turned north-south while the railroad keeps to its northwest to southeast run. Heading east, the railroad enters Wallowa County for good. The railroad continues to follow the winding path of the Wallowa River and its canyon until Minam.

To the north side of the train is Edna's Peak, at more than 3660 feet in elevation. The railroad will be squeezed between it and the Wallowa River.

46.7 MINAM – Minam sits at the junction of the Wallowa and Minam Rivers at 2547 feet above sea level, and is today a popular rafting point, with the Minam State Recreation Area nearby. The first post office opened here on June 25, 1890, with Elizabeth Richards working as postmaster. It apparently wasn't too busy as it closed on February 4, 1891. However, with the passing of the railroad through here in 1908, it reopened in June 1910, and succeeded in staying open until 1945.

The word Minam reportedly comes from the Indian name "E-mi-ne-mah," which translates to a valley or canyon where a certain species of plant thrives ("mah" means canyon or valley). If this story is true, no one really knows, but the word Minam was being used in this area as early as 1864.

Here is an interesting fact that might someday win you a trivia game. The Minam River flows out of the south end of Minam Lake. Meanwhile, the Lostine River flows out of the north end of Minam Lake, up between Matterhorn (10,004 feet) and Brown Mountain (8933 feet) south of Joseph. Both rivers eventually flow into the Wallowa River.

Minam served as a supply point for much of the area since it had both rail and road transportation. It was a regular stop for all trains, eastbound at 9:10am and westbound at 2:42pm, in 1948. A twelve-car siding once existed here, and today there is still a spur track on the river side of the mainline. There was a 48,000 gallon water tank here in 1930, was well as a freight platform. Section houses were located at Minam, with the track gang covering the route from Milepost 45.25 to Milepost 53.50 in 1930.

Minam was never a large town and it didn't host much of the timber history, although logs were shipped from the location. A three-avenue town was platted in 1907, the year before the railroad arrived. The report on the Elgin-Joseph Branch in the October 1912 issue of *The Timberman* did mention that the lumber production around Minam was developing, with the Scott Brothers, S. C. Hoff and H.A. Ackert operating mills in the area. The Minam Lumber Company operated here 1946-1951, producing as much as five million board feet a year before the mill burned. The logging was performed up the Minam River using horses. A National Forest report stated that a "splash dam was built at the Big Burn. Each day or every other day during the log drive the accumulated water behind the dam was released to raise the water in the river to drive the logs a little farther down toward the mill. Twenty to thirty days were usually required to get all the logs to the mill, and a crew of 8 or 10 men with two or three teams was required."

The railroad continues to follow the Wallowa River through narrow gorges as it approaches Minam, Oregon. Photo by Barton Jennings.

Minam did have a claim to fame as having the only stoplight ever to exist in Wallowa County. It basically served as a warning light on the old highway where it passed under the railroad, a location so narrow that some larger vehicles could not meet another vehicle. The light went away with the construction of the new road.

The railroad crosses Oregon Highway 82 here, making it a popular access point. Highway 82 is the main road between La Grande and the Grande Ronde Valley and Joseph in the Wallowa Valley. On the west side of the river and at the end of the Oregon Highway 82 bridge is Minam State Recreation Area, technically a state park administered by the Oregon Parks and Recreation Department. The park covers 600 acres and includes 22 primitive campsites, restrooms, a boat ramp, picnic areas, and a walking trail. This is often a very busy location for river floaters and fishermen.

46.9   WALLOWA RIVER BRIDGE – The railroad crosses the Wallowa River using two 60-foot and one 56-foot deck plate girder spans, plus four timber pile trestle spans. The Wallowa River starts up in the Wallowa National Forest south of Joseph and Wallowa Lake. The East Fork starts up around Petes Point (9675 feet) while the West Fork splits, with one branch coming from Frazier Lake and the other from Moccasin Lake north of Craig Mountain (9202 feet). Both forks merge just south of Wallowa Lake, and then flow into it. The Wallowa River then flows out of the north end of the lake and heads northwest to the Grande Ronde River.

For the next few miles, the railroad will be on the south bank of the Wallowa River while Highway 82 is on the north bank.

Heading east toward Joseph, the railroad passes through woods alongside the Wallowa River and into open pasture land near Harris, Oregon. Photo by Barton Jennings.

47.9 HARRIS – Located at an elevation of 2579 feet above sea level, this short siding was typically used to set off freight cars with mechanical problems before the train entered the canyon. The track is now gone, but its old grade to the south can easily be seen.

The former Harris siding can still be spotted in the brush. As at many locations along the railroad, the hillsides to the north are drier due to being in the sun all day. Photo by Barton Jennings.

48.1 DEER CREEK BRIDGE – Deer Creek is a ten-mile stream coming from the southeast. The railroad crosses it on a three-span timber pile trestle. This location is easy to find as Big Canyon Road crosses the Wallowa River and heads south into the mountains. Also here is the Big Canyon Satellite Fish Hatchery complex. This facility supports the Wallowa Fish Hatchery by collecting steelhead during the spawning season for their eggs.

A railroad water tank used to stand east of here at Milepost 49.0. Heading east, the road, river and railroad sharply curve back and forth.

50.0 **ROADSIDE PARK** – Across the Wallowa to the north is a roadside park with several signs about the area's history. This is at Mile 13 of the Wallowa River.

53.8 **WADE** – Located at an elevation of 2723 feet, today Wade is a retired station. The station area is marked by a private estate and Water Canyon Road (Milepost 54.2), which are just east of the grade for the old side track. Just east of the road crossing is a small three-span timber pile trestle over a small stream that flows out of Water Canyon.

56.3 **SEVIER** – Located at 2794 feet, Sevier marks the west end of several miles of 1% grade uphill to the east. Also to the east, the line is generally straight; to the west it is nothing but one curve after another. From Sevier to Elgin (Milepost 20.6), the line is certainly tangent-challenged with almost this entire section being made up of curves. This is because the railroad follows first the Wallowa and then the Grande Ronde Rivers as it heads west. Both rivers are used by rafters throughout the season, so wave.

Historically, Sevier has never really been much more than an 800-foot spur used by a few local shippers for livestock and timber. It was not a passenger stop in 1948, and in 1950 documents show that Sevier Spur was at Milepost 57.1. However, Sevier was the location of the last lumber mill in Wallowa County, Wallowa Forest Products. This mill was the Rogge mill, built in 1974, becoming Wallowa Forest Products in 1996, and closing about 2007, with the property now being used by several firms. Among these are Integrated Biomass Resources of Wallowa. As the company states, "we take wood that is underutilized by the traditional logging industry and turn it into useful things like firewood, poles and clean energy." The firm makes traditional firewood, processed fire logs, and fence posts and other similar products. Full-size wood can be sold to lumber companies.

The name Sevier is common in the area, with several branches of the Sevier family having lived in the area since the late 1800s. In the early 1900s, the Mc-Donald/Sevier Ranch was located on the Diamond Prairie just west of Wallowa.

Just east of the mill is a grade crossing with Upper Diamond Lane (Milepost 56.9). The open land to the southeast is Diamond Prairie. Diamond Prairie was one of the first areas settled by whites, starting about 1871. At the time, the land was the property of Chief Joseph of the Nez Percé Tribe. The valley was described in a 1957 article in the *Chief Joseph Herald* "Memoirs of Alexander B. And Sarah Jane Findley." It stated that "Diamond Prairie like a huge emerald diamond lay in the immediate foreground. Grand evergreen clad mountains crowned with snow-capped peaks towered like mighty sentinels guarding the valley on the South and Southwest, and on the South East the rugged Seven Devils were mirrored in a sky blue background, while on the East were miles and miles of bunch grass covered hills and valleys which ran on and on in undulating waves to finally meet the horizon in a field of azure blue." Much of this prairie is today used for agriculture and homes.

58.9 BEAR CREEK BRIDGE – Bear Creek is the most common creek name in Oregon, with at least 123 streams with that name in the state. There are at least five in Wallowa County alone. This Bear Creek comes from the slopes of Bald Mountain, about 15 miles to the south in the Eagle Cap Wilderness area. Early settlers in the Wallowa Valley found many bears along this stream. Reportedly, the bears were heavily hunted as the cattle became a favorite meal of the bears.

The upper part of Bear Creek is followed by Bear Creek Trail, officially Forest Service Trail #1653. As described by the Forest Service, "views along the trail gradually change from flower filled meadows to scattered pines and a dense forest canopy." Camping and fishing is also available along the trail.

59.5 WALLOWA (WO) – Originally called Gate City, the first post office in Wallowa County opened here in 1873. However, the post office wasn't actually in Wallowa, but was at the bridge over Whiskey Creek east of here. Wallowa was named for (1) the valley, (2) the mountains, or (3) the river. You choose as different sources credit different features. What we do know is that a "wallowa" is probably a part of a willow fish trap used by local Natives, an indication of the good fishing found in the area streams. The Nez Percé called this area Hi-paah, meaning "bear robbing salmon cache." The town is at an elevation of 2913 (some sources say 2950) feet.

Wallowa was platted in 1889 and incorporated as a city in 1899. Its population in the 2010 census was 808. It is generally described as a small town that serves the local farming and ranching business twelve months out of the year, and the heavy tourist business during summer and fall. Wallowa is also known as the one-time home of the brothers Amos Marsh, Jr. and Frank Wayne Marsh, football players at Oregon State University, and later in the professional ranks. Amos was a running back in the National Football League for the Dallas Cowboys and Detroit Lions while

Frank played defensive back in the American Football League for the San Diego Chargers.

The Lumber Business

Wallowa was the site of the first large-scale lumber mill in the county. It soon was just one of a large number of mills operating along the line, cutting the timber easily found on the nearby hillsides. The October 1912 report on the Elgin-Joseph Branch, found in *The Timberman*, had a detailed report on the lumber business at Wallowa. The report made it clear that timber cutting and milling had started in earnest with the arrival of the railroad in 1908. While there were reports of small mills operating to serve local business, the railroad allowed the lumber to reach national markets. This timber was in fact a major justification of the construction of the railroad. In 1912, one small mill, the Bear Creek Lumber Company operated by the Plauss Brothers, had not turned a wheel that year. Also that year, John McDonald was operating two small mills, which between them cut about 2,500,000 board feet of lumber. It was noted that with the local growth, much of this lumber was sold locally. It was also noted that John McDonald had just been elected to represent the Twenty-fourth District in the Oregon State Legislature.

The Timberman also had an interesting comment about the area box industry. It stated that "recent early frosts in Utah have cut down the tomato crop very much. The apple production in the Grande Ronde will be heavy."

Nibley-Mimnaugh Lumber Company

The major Wallowa mill in operation at the time was the Nibley-Mimnaugh Lumber Company, which started building its mill in 1908, and as reported by the *Wallowa County Chieftain*, started with a full crew during April 1911. At the time, the company manufactured wooden crates, or "boxes," for the Eastern Oregon, Idaho, Utah and Colorado markets. It also manufactured lumber for larger markets such as Chicago, all in a mill with a capacity of 50,000 feet daily. In 1912, the company shipped almost fifteen million feet of lumber, mostly pine. To move the timber to the mill, the company had three miles of logging railroad and operated a Heisler locomotive.

James Mimnaugh, logging engineer for the company, began buying timber in the area in 1901. Construction on a box factory, planing mill and sawmill began in 1908, using land between the railroad and the Wallowa River, where Evans Park is located today. Some of the foundations are still visible. The existing Bear Creek Lumber mill was hired to provide the original construction materials. Over the next decade, the company expanded its logging operations to include eighteen miles of mainline, plus a number of short spur tracks. The line went up Dry Creek, northwest of Wallowa and east of Smith Mountain. Dry Creek flows into the Wallowa River west of Sevier.

Late in 1922, James Mimnaugh died, leaving his stock in the company to his family. On August 2, 1923, the Bowman-Hicks Lumber Company of Kansas City agreed to buy Nibley-Mimnaugh for the sum of $1,150,000 and the assumption by the purchaser of the seller's liabilities and contracts. Payments were to be made as follows: $100,000 at once, $350,000 upon ratification of the agreement by the stockholders, and the balance in annual installments over a period of five years.

Bowman-Hicks Lumber Company

Nibley-Mimnaugh was not the first lumber company in the area to be bought by Bowman-Hicks. In 1922-1923, Palmer Lumber sold out to Bowman-Hicks Lumber Company. Bowman-Hicks was a large lumber company owned by William C. Bowman and based in Kansas City (Bowman's house there is still a tourist and historical draw) but with mills from Missouri to Louisiana. This mill was known as Mill #2. With the expansion due to the purchase of the company, more timber was needed, and the company built more temporary rail lines into the mountains to serve such camps as Promise and Maxville. Some of these trains ran over the Joseph Branch to reach mills with lumber from the logging camps.

The line up to Promise and Maxville from Wallowa only lasted about ten years. The rail line reached Maxville about 1926 and then kept going north into the Grande Ronde River area at Promise. For those who are curious, Promise is located about 17 miles north of Wallowa up past Dry Creek near Sickfoot Creek (named for local settler David Rochester, who was named Sickfoot by the Indians because of his clubfoot). Promise Road runs along the route of the original logging railroad from near Wallowa all the way to the Grande Ronde River twenty miles to the north. John C. Philips and W. Mann settled near what became Promise about 1891 and took up homesteads. Mann reportedly called the place "Promised Land" and "Land of Promise," and when a post office was established on December 22, 1896, it took the name of Promise.

Maxville was a good-sized town about two-thirds of the way to Promise on the northeast side of Akers Butte. Maxville had a store, school, church, sawmill, and many other businesses. Maxville was a logging town with an interesting background created by the need to cut timber. When Bowman-Hicks bought the Palmer Logging operations, they brought their existing laborers from the south. This created a conflict between the whites and the newly arrived blacks, causing Maxville to have what was reportedly the first segregated school system in Oregon. When logging in the area ended during the 1930s, the buildings (many of which were portable) were sold off and many became outbuildings in Wallowa. The railroad was also quickly abandoned. Today about the only building to mark the site of Maxville is the old logging supervisor's cabin. For those who want the entire story, there is a book on the market about the town.

Until Bowman-Hicks closed down the logging railroad during the late 1930s, the company used a large fleet of geared locomotives. Four of them were previously owned by Palmer Lumber. These were Palmer Lumber Shay locomotives #1 (cn 1894), #2 (cn 2144), #3 (cn 2845), and #4 (cn 3008).

For Bowman-Hicks, five additional locomotives are typically shown as having worked on the logging railroads. The first was Heisler #1, formerly operated by Nibley-Mimnaugh. A Heisler was a geared locomotive that had two cylinders canted inwards to power a drive shaft in the center of the locomotive frame. The Heisler was the last of the three geared steam locomotives designed and was first built by the Dunkirk Engineering Company, then the Stearns Manufacturing Company, and finally by the Heisler Locomotive Works until production ended in 1941. This locomotive was a 2-truck model with construction number 1085, built in May 1905.

Bowman-Hicks #2 was a small 2-truck Shay (cn 814) built in August 1903. #3 was a 2-truck Heisler (cn 1151) manufactured in August 1909 that formerly was owned by Nibley-Mimnaugh Lumber. #4 was another 2-truck Heisler (cn 1377), this one built in June 1918. The final locomotive, Bowman-Hicks #7, was a 2-truck Heisler locomotive built in 1903 and formerly operated by Morrison-Knudsen. It had construction number 1084.

During World War II, Bowman-Hicks Lumber was able to get a number of their most valuable employees exempt from the draft. The company had a contract to cut timbers for military boat construction and with tools and replacement parts scarce during the war, Bowman-Hicks had to rely upon the skills and experience of its employees to keep the aging mill operating.

In November 1945, Bowman-Hicks sold its mill and timber property to J. Herbert Bate Company of New York City. The firm had long operated in North Carolina and was looking for new timber to harvest. The *Wallowa County Chieftain* of June 23, 1949, stated that the payroll of the J. Herbert Bate mill was the largest in Wallowa County, showing the importance of the mill to the region. In November 1953, the mill's planer complex burned, reducing the mill's output. By 1962, J. Herbert Bate was having trouble with the mill and began lowering the pay, leading to a strike vote by the workers in June 1962. The strike lasted more than a year, and soon after the strike ended, the firm announced the mill's closure on Valentine's Day in

1964. Almost immediately, the mill was sold to Boise Cascade, which dismantled the facility. The property of the Bates mill was soon sold by auction.

The Railroad at Wallowa

A group gathers at the "Elk Train" as it stops at the Wallowa two-story station in 1912. Photo by William L. Finley from the William L. Finley Photographs Collection, circa 1900-1940, The Oregon Historical Society Library.

According to several sources, the first train over the newly built railroad arrived in Wallowa on September 21, 1908. Reports are that the celebration included an excursion train from La Grande to Wallowa. Between 1500 and 2000 people gathered with much fanfare to celebrate the arrival of the first passenger train in Wallowa. The railroad actually doesn't go through Wallowa, instead it loops around the northeast side of town, following the Wallowa River.

The railroad built a 2400-foot siding here, located to the south of the mainline. There is also a wye track here to the south. The location was busy enough that there was generally a daytime operator assigned to Wallowa. There was also water supplied from a column connected to city water, a 4-pen stockyard, and a freight platform. In 1948, Wallowa was a regular stop for all trains, eastbound at 9:50am and westbound at 2:10pm. During the mid-1980s, Union Pacific based one of their maintenance section gangs on the line here. In 1930, there were section houses here for the workers, who at that time maintained the track from Milepost 53.5 to Milepost 63.5.

59.7 CLEAR WATER DITCH BRIDGE – It takes a twenty-foot beam open deck bridge to cross this channel. Clear Water Ditch takes water out of the Lostine River about five miles southeast of Wallowa. It then flows west and then north to this point where it flows back into the Wallowa River. Along the route it serves as an irrigation canal. Union Pacific records show this canal to be Mill Ditch.

The east switch of the Wallowa railyard complex is just west of this bridge.

59.8 WALLOWA RIVER BRIDGE – The railroad crosses the river on a seven-span timber pile trestle, with skewed concrete piers.

To the northeast is Tick Hill, elevation 3533 feet. This area is part of 320 acres of land still owned by the Nez Percé tribe and used for their annual Tamkaliks Celebration, held every July. The event is held at the large arena at the base of the hill, visible from the tracks. The arena is designed to shade spectators observing dancing and drumming by descendants of the original inhabitants of waláwa, the Wallowa country.

Great views of the Wallowa area are available from the top of Tick Hill, which can be climbed using an established trail that begins just northeast of the Tamkaliks Celebration arena.

60.3 WHISKEY CREEK BRIDGE – In 1872, several traders brought a supply of whiskey by pack train from Walla Walla and began to trade it to the Indians for Indian goods. Local residents became very alarmed and went to the camp to put a stop to the business. A three-cornered fight ensued (settlers, Indians and traders), which was won by the settlers. The kegs were broken and the whiskey ran into the stream, which has been known as Whiskey Creek ever since.

Whiskey Creek flows west from the Powwatka Ridge, the north-south ridge that runs just north of here. The word Powwatka reportedly means "high, cleared ground." The railroad only requires a three-span trestle to cross Whiskey Creek, demonstrating how the lower ridges to the north don't collect the rain and snowfall that the higher mountains to the south do.

East of here, the railroad passes through miles of irrigated farm and ranch land. There are few curves, but the grade continues to climb at almost one percent. The views vary from the green valley to the dry grass-covered hills to the north, and the tree-covered mountains to the south.

62.2 BAKER ROAD GRADE CROSSING – Here, the railroad passes through several small farm complexes. Not far to the south is the Wallowa River and its junction with the Lostine River. The Lostine River is more than thirty miles long, and forms at an elevation of 7373 feet from Minam Lake deep in the Eagle Cap Wilderness. In 1988, the Lostine River was listed as Wild and Scenic, with the five miles immediately below Minam Lake as "Wild" and the next eleven miles as "Recreational."

The river flows northward out of the mountains to here, losing 3500 feet in elevation before leaving the National Forest. The river was once a major Chinook salmon run. However, the loss of water from the river due to irrigation canals basically eliminated the fish from the stream. During the late 1990s, an effort by the Nez Percé and the Oregon Water Trust led to more stable water flows. The result has been the return of a sizeable spring Chinook salmon run.

63.7 IRRIGATION CANAL BRIDGE – A single span timber pile trestle is used to cross this canal, located just west of the Warnock Road grade crossing. Rainfall in this valley is about a foot a year, but the surrounding mountains can receive heavy snowfall. Irrigation is important for much of the area's farming and ranching, and a number of irrigation canals crisscross the valley.

64.7 BEAVER CREEK BRIDGE – There are streams named Beaver Creek in almost every county in Oregon. Beaver were very numerous through the early days in Oregon. Diaries from the early 1800s show counts as high as 735 pelts taken in three weeks on only two small streams. No wonder Oregon has so many Beaver Creeks and so few beavers. The railroad crosses the stream on a five-span timber pile trestle.

65.0 WALLOWA RIVER BRIDGE – At high water, the Wallowa River can be about one-third mile wide here, but can easily be waded during much of the year. The railroad crosses it on a one-span timber pile trestle (64.8), five-span steel pile trestle (65.0), and one-span

(65.1) timber pile trestle. The main channel is crossed with the steel pile trestle.

Heading east towards Joseph, the tracks are actually heading due south.

67.5 LOSTINE (NS) – The City of Lostine is located about a mile to the south, located on the banks of the Lostine River, which is often identified as the South Fork of the Wallowa River. The community was named by W. R. Laughlin, an early settler, after his former home of Lostine, Kansas. The post office was opened in August of 1878 with Laughlin as postmaster. Shortly afterwards, Laughlin left the valley for some reason and his wife took over the duties at the post office. Although a few stores and a blacksmith had located here, it wasn't until 1884 that the town was actually platted for further development.

Lostine is located in an open valley north of the Eagle Cap Wilderness Area. Here a WURR locomotive passes by the site of the town of Evans. Photo by Barton Jennings.

Lostine was located on the Joseph & Elgin Stage Line route, giving it some importance. The town burned several times in the 1890s, but the presence of the Lostine Flouring Mill Company kept the community going. The community was incorporated in 1903. Unlike many other area towns, Lostine never developed a large lumber industry. The February 14, 1909, *Wallowa County Chieftain* reported that two new sawmills were to start at Lostine. *The Timberman* (October 1912) stated that "Q. E. Gwynne Lumber Co. of Lostine have their new planing mill in operation. The mill is located about two miles from the planing mill. The company cut two million feet this season. Next season double this amount will be cut. Manager Gwynne says his shop was sold in Chicago. He reports plenty of orders."

Early reports show that Lostine was a typical rural community, with general and drug stores, a butcher shop, blacksmith shop and livery, boarding house and hotel, millinery, planing mill, and sawmill. The population of Lostine has changed little since its early days. In 1910, the census showed that the population was 230. It reached a low of 176 in 1930, and then peaked at 263 in 2000. Today, the population is estimated to be 213.

Evans

As surveys were made to build the railroad to Joseph, it became obvious that Lostine was not on the logical route along the Wallowa River. Citizens of Lostine met several times with the railroad surveyors and engineers in an attempt to change the route, but they refused to make any financial payments to cover the additional costs.

This is the former one-story Lostine station, as seen in 1912. The station was actually located at Evans, Oregon. Photo by William L. Finley from the William L. Finley Photographs Collection, circa 1900-1940, The Oregon Historical Society Library.

In 1907, the railroad built north of the town of Lostine, but at least the railroad developed a siding for local business. There was once a 5-pen stockyard here for livestock, often sheep around Lostine. The single-story station had the typical freight platform, and there were section houses for the track gang responsible for maintaining the track between Mileposts 63.5 and 74.25. A siding that is 1885 feet long still exists on the south side of the mainline. This area is on a constant 0.8% grade heading toward Joseph, at an elevation of 3264 feet. It was a regular stop for all trains in 1948, eastbound at 10:07am and westbound at 1:53pm.

Because the railroad was some distance away from Lostine, the few major industries that required rail service located north of town. The remains of a grain elevator still stand. The area was known as Jim Town (note the Jim Town Road crossing at Milepost 67.1) for James Haun, one of the first to move his house and other buildings to the new railroad siding. Haun platted the town of Evans, reportedly named for Mrs. Louisa Evans, the wife of Sam Wade and the sister of James Evans. What adds some confusion to this naming is that nearby Evans Creek and Evans Meadows was named for another James Evans, who lived in the area years earlier. Even though the local community was Evans, the railroad still called the siding and passenger train stop Lostine. There was an Evans post office here from 1913 until 1940. Today, Evans is an unincorporated community.

68.7 CROSS COUNTRY DITCH BRIDGE – This ditch actually connects the Wallowa and Lostine Rivers. It is one of thirteen irrigation ditches that take water out of the Lostine River. It takes water from the river 5.3 miles above where the river flows into the Wallowa River, and distributes it to farms across the valley. The railroad crosses the irrigation ditch using a single-span timber pile trestle.

69.8 WADE GULCH LANE – Heading east, the railroad starts running on the north side of Highway 82, often squeezed between a hillside and the highway to the south, and the Wallowa River to the north. Past the narrow cut at Wade Point, the landscape again opens up. With Wade Point and Wade Gulch here, it is obvious that the Wade family has ranched in this area for multiple generations.

72.5 **GWYNNE** – Look for where there is a grade crossing between the railroad and Oregon Highway 82. This location was known as Gwynne or Gynne Siding during the 1910s. It was named for Quincy and Jerome Gynne who erected a planing mill on land leased from Fred Fitzpatrick. A saw mill owned by the same family cut lumber for the planer at the upper end of Sheep Ridge. Both mills were sold to A. Hackbarth as his Lapwai Lumber Company. Hackbarth built a commissary to support the operation. In 1919, the two mills were moved to near Enterprise. Unfortunately, when the Gynnes sold the mills, they left behind a great deal of debt. Reportedly, this was not the first time they had played this trick. For several years, Hackbarth had to fight off financial claims against his lumber company.

For the railroad, the construction of the planer was enough to build a siding here. However, there was never a post office and the location was not a regular passenger stop. To handle the mail service, sacks of mail were dropped off and picked up by trains. Not long after the planer was moved, the tracks also came out. Today, this is simply another retired station, this one located at an elevation of about 3500 feet.

It should be noted that Mr. Hackbarth had another claim to fame in the area. In July 1918, he announced the construction of the O.K. Theatre in Enterprise. The theater was as modern as they came, using a sloping floor which would allow everyone in the theater to have a good view, five safety exits, and steam heat. The grand opening was on Saturday, January 25, 1919. It also was the first theater in the region to show a talking movie. This was the R.K.O. picture *Street Girl* which was shown during September 1929.

72.6 WALLOWA RIVER BRIDGE – It again takes two bridges to cross the river, a six-span and a two-span (72.58) timber pile trestle. The larger bridge crosses the main channel to the east while the smaller bridge is there to handle high water in the spring. The railroad is basically aligned east-west at this location.

75.1 FREEL – This is another retired railroad station, this one at 3629 feet above sea level. A short 300-foot siding existed here into the late 1970s. On February 19, 1986, the track just west of here at Milepost 74.5 washed out during a sudden spring thaw. This is actually a fairly common activity in this area as the streams and rivers tend to wander where they want to during times of high water. Interestingly enough, the next day a hard freeze caused a number of frost heaves (raised track due to expanding, frozen ground moisture) just east of here to Marble. To handle this mess, a 5 mph slow order was placed throughout this entire area, making the maintenance-of-way department again the source of much train crew griping.

A WURR freight locomotive is passing through the pastures that once were Freel, in this May 2004 photo. Photo by Barton Jennings.

75.2 WALLOWA RIVER BRIDGE – This is a five-span timber pile trestle. Heading towards Joseph, the railroad turns to the southeast, crosses the Wallowa River, and moves away from Highway 82. The railroad is on a steady grade of between 0.8% and 1.0% upward toward Joseph.

75.9 MARBLE – Marble is a retired station at 3663 feet in elevation. It was located where the small one-span timber trestle exists today. The Black Marble & Lime Company was once nearby, and the grade once used to serve the quarry can be seen to the south.

The black limestone in the mountains to the south apparently was known long before the railroad got here, and there have been a number of reports about the deposits in sources such as *The Mineral Resources of Oregon* (November 1914), *Nonmetallic Mineral Resources of Eastern Oregon* (by Bernard N. Moore in 1937), and others. Some of the early information can be conflicting, but the Oregon Black Marble Company was first created to develop the property. Dr. J. W. Barnard, who manufactured medicines for human and animal consumption in nearby Joseph, owned a large percentage of the company. A National Register report on Dr. Barnard provided much detail about the operations.

> *"A new draw kiln was built in June, 1918. It was located in a meadow on the west bank of the Wallowa River about one mile north of Enterprise. At this location was a cooperage shop where barrels were made in which to ship the lime. This industrial plant had two large, metal retorts or vertical furnaces which rise about sixty*

feet into the air. The kiln is made of fire brick, incased in a sheet steel cylinder. The black marble was dumped in at the top and drawn out pure white lime at the bottom, after burning. It was carried on trucks to the warehouse where it remained in bulk until shipped. From the time the hard marble left the quarry until it reached the railroad cars, every movement was downhill. The handling was easy because of gravity."

The firm was apparently never very profitable, and some debts were paid directly by Dr. Barnard. The firm was reorganized as the Joseph Black Marble Company, which went bankrupt in the 1920s. According to *Nonmetallic Mineral Resources of Eastern Oregon*, the Black Marble & Lime Company was organized in February 1925. Records show that in 1925, the company claimed 159.767 acres as the Black Beauty and Black Susan Placers. Moore stated that the "quarry is in a dense forest high on the face of the Wallowa Mountains at an altitude of nearly 7,000 feet. It is reached by a steep narrow road over which limestone is hauled from the quarry to the mill." Bernard N. Moore visited the quarry in 1931 and wrote that much of the deposit was being mined using a tunnel. He also provided a detailed description of the operation.

"The limestone is shot down, loaded by hand into cars, and dumped into storage bins. The original plans called for the erection of an aerial tram about 4 miles long to carry the limestone to the mill, but insufficient money was raised and a caterpillar tractor and trailers were used as a tem-

*porary substitute. The trailers weighed 15
tons apiece and carried 10-ton loads. They
were hauled over a long, narrow, steep road
7 miles to the mill. The limestone is now
hauled by 5-ton trucks."*

*"The mill is near Enterprise and has a
capacity of about 10,000 tons of quicklime
a year. Its total production to June 1931 had
been about 7,000 tons. The plant consists
of a weighing house where the limestone is
dumped and loaded into tared cars, which
carry it up an incline and dump it into any
one of three vertical kilns. The warehouse
is on the hillside below the kilns, and the
finished product can be loaded directly into
the cars."*

The quarry itself was up Murray Creek in an area
known as the Murray Saddle of the Hurricane Divide,
located just northwest of Ruby Peak. In 1935, this was
within the boundaries of the Wallowa National Forest, but the Black Marble & Lime Company owned
land along Murray Creek just outside the national
forest boundary. The site can be accessed from Lime
Quarry Road, which was used for several decades to
move limestone off of the mountain. A report within
the 2003 Wallowa County Comprehensive Land Use
Plan states that the Black Marble & Lime Company smelter has been inoperative for many years and
that most of the structure has been dismantled and
removed from the site.

76.1 SPRING CREEK BRIDGE – This small stream
drains much of the pasture in this area. It can be a

rushing stream at some times of the year. The railroad uses a four-span timber pile trestle bridge to cross it.

Just east of here the railroad crosses Fish Hatchery Lane. Not much further east is the Wallowa Hatchery, originally opened in 1920 as a resident trout hatchery. It was renovated in 1985 and is used for adult collection, spawning, acclimation and release of summer steelhead, as well as the production of trout. There is a visitor center, and the area around the hatchery has been developed into a small wildlife area, featuring a trail that leads to several viewing areas. Spring Creek flows through the site and is dammed to form a small wildlife pond.

76.8 HURRICANE CREEK BRIDGE – It takes a four-span timber pile trestle to cross this creek. The creek was named by C. A. Smith in the early 1880s. He explored the creek after a big storm and found a great many trees blown down. The first sawmill built in the Wallowa Valley was built on this creek about 1878 by E. V. Cohorn.

77.0 WALLOWA RIVER BRIDGE – Do you get the idea that the line is sharing the valley with this river? The railroad crosses it here on two bridges, one at 76.9 (two-span timber pile trestle) and the main one at 77.0 (three-span timber pile trestle). In this area, the river is basically a series of small channels that change and move based upon the level of the river.

WURR 4508 crosses one of a number of Wallowa River Bridges near Enterprise in 2004. Photo by Barton Jennings.

77.6 ENTERPRISE (PR) – Welcome to "Tom-mah-talk-ke-sin-mah," located at an elevation of 3753 feet above sea level. The Native name means white, fluffy, or alkali soils. This area was a natural mineral lick used by wildlife, meaning it was a great hunting area. White settlers discovered the minerals and used them in their farm activities.

This is the northern end of the Wallowa River Valley, the traditional homeland of the Wal-lam-wat-kain (Wallowa) band of the Nez Percé. This area was a designated Nez Percé reservation, but white settlers began moving into the area by 1872, initially to graze cattle in the lush summer pastures. Ore discoveries in other parts of the northwest, and demand for ranch lands, finally resulted in the forced relocation of the Wallowa band in 1877. New settlements began almost immediately.

During the 1880s, officers of the Island City Mercantile & Milling Company (ICM&MC), from near

La Grande, started contacting communities in this area about expanding the company's holdings. Both Lostine and Wallowa refused to cooperate. However, John Zurcher and R. F. Stubblefield of Bennett Flats saw an opportunity with the proposal. In 1886, they platted a community using the name Franklin, and then replatted the area as Wallowa City on June 21, 1887. As a part of the plan, the ICM&MC received several lots diagonally across the street from the designed "Public Square" for a store, and a block near Prairie Creek between SW 2nd and 3rd streets on Greenwood Street for a new flourmill. This led to the incorporation of the Enterprise Flouring Mill.

The name Enterprise came about because the post office refused the name Wallowa City because of nearby Wallowa. One story states that a meeting was called to select a new name. It was held in the tent of the new mercantile company, and possible names for the new community were suggested, including some of the old ones like Bennett Flat and Franklin, as well as Fairfield. Apparently, the decision became quite an issue, to the point that Stubblefield remarked, "Well, it will probably be an enterprising little town, anyway." Poof – Enterprise was born, or so goes the story. A post office was established at Enterprise on November 9, 1887, with Catherine Akin handling the postmaster duties. The same year, J. Church opened a two-story school house here. Enterprise became the Wallowa county seat in 1888, thanks to the efforts of the ICM&MC. On June 14, 1888, the name of Enterprise became official, and it was incorporated in 1889 with Church as its mayor.

The flour mill opened in 1888 and had a capacity of 50 barrels a day, attracting farmers and ranchers that purchased flour or brought in their wheat to trade or sell. This made the south side of town the industrial area. The mercantile building and Wallowa National Bank (the first in the county) made downtown a busy location, the social center of the region. When the railroad built through the south side of Enterprise in 1908 (the first train arrived in September to the gathering of hundreds), more industry was attracted to this part of town.

WURR 4508 passes the grain elevator at Enterprise in 2004. Photo by Barton Jennings.

The 1910s were good times for Enterprise. Besides the lumber mills, Enterprise also featured the Enterprise Mercantile and Milling Company and its flour mill, the Enterprise Water Company and its area ponds, a planing mill, lots of general stores, a steam laundry, lots of attorneys, and everything else that a somewhat civilized community needed.

The 1920s began a downturn in the history of Enterprise as the lumber business began its slow decline. In December 1926, the Enterprise Flour Mill burned down and was not replaced. The Enterprise City Park exists there now. The East Oregon Lumber Company's mill went into receivership in the fall of 1928. The O.K. Theatre went into foreclosure in 1932, and sold, becoming the Vista Theatre.

Today, Enterprise is the center of Wallowa County, housing most of the hotels, restaurants, and just plain general businesses in the area. When the railroad arrived in 1908, it built along the south edge of town, creating a building boom in the area. An article in the local newspaper reported on the start of passenger train service. In the November 14, 1908, issue, an article stated that Enterprise to La Grande passenger service had started that morning at 8:30am when a train of two coaches, baggage and mail car, and engine No. 103 left town. The article also stated that the train had arrived the night before. It also stated that the service would probably be extended to Joseph in a week or ten days.

Enterprise was a regular stop for all trains in 1948. For #304, it was a scheduled stop at 11:00am. For the westbound #305, 1:30pm was the scheduled departure time. Today, several grain elevators and related businesses are in the South Depot Street area along the tracks where these trains used to stop many years ago.

The railroad had the typical freight platform at Enterprise, handling smaller shipments for local businesses. The railroad used the city water system and had a column alongside the tracks that could be used by steam locomotives. Enterprise was also in the middle of livestock country, and there was an 11-pen stockyard here. Finally, the railroad built several section houses here for the track gang that repaired the track between Milepost 74.25 and Joseph.

Enterprise is the business center fot the region, and many of the companies stand next to the tracks. Photo by Barton Jennings.

The Enterprise depot originally was located near the corner of Depot and Alamo Streets. The gambrel-roof depot was completed in 1909, located several blocks south of Main Street on Depot Street, formerly SW 1st Street. The depot featured a second story to house the station agent and his family. While no longer in Enterprise, it does still exist. In 1972 it was moved to just north of Joseph out on the main highway. After going through several owners and uses, it became the *Depot Gardens*, surrounded by gardens and a G-scale model train. Most recently, it is *The Depot*, a bed-and-breakfast that features a caboose that can be rented. The caboose is former Chicago, Burlington & Quincy 13610, manufactured in September 1967 by Morrison International. It was last Burlington Northern 10108, and still carries this paint.

The Enterprise depot has been moved to a site north of Joseph, as shown here in 2004. Photo by Barton Jennings.

The original Enterprise depot is shown in this 1912 photo of the elk resettlement. Photo by William L. Finley from the William L. Finley Photographs Collection, circa 1900-1940, The Oregon Historical Society Library.

East Oregon Lumber Company

As with most of the towns along this part of the railroad, Enterprise had its lumber business. The October 1912 *The Timberman* did not list any major mills here at the time, but a number of small mills were noted. These included Thomas A. Morgan's City Planing Mill, J. R. McCoy's small mill and box factory, and a few other mills in the hills around the area. However, it was predicted that a large mill would be there soon because "there is quite a body of timber land in the National Forest tributary to Enterprise, which will be eventually manufactured at this point."

The June 18, 1914, issue of the *Enterprise Record Chieftain* had an announcement that a sawmill was to be built at Enterprise. The town of Enterprise had a reputation of providing land to those who would build and create jobs. In 1914, the East Oregon Lumber Company (EOLC) received "80 acres in the heart of the city" to build a two-band sawmill with a 100,000 board feet daily capacity, plus a right-of-way for a logging railroad and $50,000 in stock subscriptions. The August 15, 1914, issue of *The St. Louis Lumberman* had a sizeable article about the company. It stated that the company had acquired 120 million feet of government timber in Wallowa County, and that a 12-mile railroad would be built, with plans to extend it to several mills at Flora, north from Enterprise near the Washington State border.

The East Oregon Lumber Company was owned by the Jackson Lumber Company of Kansas City, one of several companies that Jackson Lumber owned in the west. A report stated that the machine shop and engine house foundation were completed and work was progressing on other foundations and the mill pond by October 10, 1914. A front page report in the *Enterprise Record Chieftain* of October 29, 1914, covered the line's construction and stated that lumber for the machine shop and roundhouse was ordered from the Nibley-Mimnaugh Lumber Company in Wallowa. On Sunday, March 14, 1915, a special excursion train ran up the logging railroad, using seats built on construction flat cars. Soon, logs were arriving at the mill and the company had opened a company store in Enterprise. The first log was cut at the new mill on November 22, 1915. More than 300 workers were employed by the firm.

The EOLC was naturally a common topic in the *Enterprise Record Chieftain*, later the *Wallowa County Chieftain*. The EOLC sawmill burned down in August 1919. A new, more modern mill was built and opened in July 1920. A headline in the March 3, 1921, issue stated that the mill's payroll was more than $50,000, and the October 6, 1921, issue reported on the mill being closed so it could be overhauled. The mill was again open and running with a full crew by July 1922. The following year was a good one for the lumber company as it was setting volume records, including moving more than 1000 railcars of timber. As with many of the regional lumber companies, the late 1920s were not kind. The company was not able to compete, and efforts were made to cut wages, resulting in a number of actions by the workers. After several closings and openings, the mill was closed in July 1928. The company entered bankruptcy and a receiver was assigned to EOLC in May 1928. The newspaper later had a large announcement that the East Oregon Lumber Company bankruptcy sale was scheduled for October 17, 1928. With the sale, the mill became the property of the Oregon White Pine Lumber Company of

Kansas City, while somehow, the Enterprise Logging Company wound up with the ownership of the logging railroad and equipment.

The East Oregon Lumber Company Logging Railroad

The East Oregon Lumber Company began operations here in 1915, employing 500 in the mill and logging. With the boom in logging, the population of Wallowa County jumped to its all-time peak of 12,000 in 1916. To get to the timber, the East Oregon Lumber Company built several logging lines into the nearby mountains. The first grading on the line to the north along Trout Creek began Wednesday, July 8, 1921. Construction began in the Bank's pasture in Enterprise, in soil that was described as gummy and cloggy, the sod stringy, and the conditions difficult to cut and fill. The first public excursion over the line happened the next March 14th when "half a hundred" rode a construction train from the roundhouse to the end of track in T. D. Bonnel's field.

The logging railroad went north out of Enterprise, following Trout Creek, much of the same route as today's Enterprise-Lewiston Highway, Oregon Highway 3. It passed through farms and ranch country, but little else. Among the few named locations was Sled Springs. Sled Springs was named for a broken-down sled abandoned by James Alford and George Allen about 1883. The sled remained near the springs in ruins for many years, becoming a local landmark. You can find the site of Sled Springs by driving north on Highway 3 out of Enterprise. After going 20.5 miles north of Highway 82 to near Kuhn Ridge Road (named for Henry and Dave Kuhn, who were some of the first to range cattle here), the site is on your left in the middle of a series of wet-weather creeks.

A logging base was established at Patterson where a mill was operated, and the railroad included a wye track. Camp 1 was also in this area. Patterson was near the top of the grade where Davis Creek forms to flow north. Eight miles of track was built along Davis Creek for logging, then moved to build a line east into the Swamp Creek basin on the west side of Elk Mountain in 1918. This route is still used as a rough four-wheel drive road into the mountains.

The Swamp Creek line lasted through 1923 when it was removed and a line built up Davis Creek and then up into the mountains, reaching Kuhn Ridge by early 1927. Much of this last work required significant amounts of earthwork and a number of timber trestles. Reports indicate that modern steam ditchers were used, creating an attraction for many in the area. The *Enterprise Record Chieftain* had something about the lumber company and its railroad in almost every issue. Reports on the company's logging camps (at least ten are mentioned) and rail operations cover everything from the housing conditions to the merchandise in the company stores.

To work the various logging lines, East Oregon Lumber at first used second hand steam locomotives. These traditional locomotives had trouble with the poorly built grade. However, in 1919, the company acquired a new Shay locomotive #5 that had been built for the US Spruce Production Company, which was formed to log spruce for the aircraft needed by the US Army during World War I. With the ending of the war, the locomotive wasn't needed and was sold. The locomotive was an oil-burning Shay C70-3 (cn3011), meaning that it weighed about 70 tons and had three trucks under the engine. A Shay was not like a normal steam locomotive with side rods being pushed by steam cylinders on each side of the locomotive to turn the wheels. Instead, a Shay has a set of vertical cylinders on the engineer's side of the locomotive which drives a drive shaft which connects to every wheel of the locomotive. The design allows the engine to be very flexible and powerful and is able to haul great loads at low speeds over very rough track.

A second geared locomotive used on the line was Heisler #2, built in February 1916 as construction number 1325. Because of the distance between the timber and the mill at Enterprise, several traditional steam locomotives were also acquired. One was Baldwin construction number 45248, a 2-8-2 built in February 1917. EOLC #3 later became Columbia & Colitz #102, then the property of the Weyerhaeuser Timber Company.

One other Shay is known to have been in Enterprise, but not doing the normal work of a logging steam engine. Oregon Lumber Company/Sumpter Valley #102 was a B24-2 Shay (cn1885) built in 1907 for use south of Baker, Oregon. When it was scrapped in 1945, its boiler was sold to Eagle Cap Laundry in Enterprise to make hot water and steam for the operation.

Oregon White Pine Lumber Company

The Oregon White Pine Lumber Company was another firm based in Kansas City, Missouri, and was created to buy the East Oregon Lumber Company mill. It should be noted that the term Oregon white pine was used as a regional name for ponderosa pine. There were plans to reopen the mill in 1929, but back taxes owed by the EOLC, the lack of ownership of the logging railroad, and the beginning of the Great Depression delayed the opening. The mill operated off and on through the 1930s, generally using timber hauled in by truck off of the Oregon White Pine Lumber lands, and by independent contractors. Maps from 1935 don't show the railroad, but do show that much of the land was owned by the Oregon White Pine Lumber Company, the firm that bought the EOLC in 1928. Those who drive Highway 3 can occasionally see the old railroad grade.

What became known as the Murrey sawmill opened in 1940, and was called a "big concern" on October 31, 1941, by the *Chieftain*. In May 1945, the Murrey sawmill was sold to the Mt. Emily Lumber Company, which operated in La Grande from 1920 until 1956. The firm had been buying timber in the area for several years, and participated in a number of national forest timber auctions through the 1950s. As stated in a forestry report, the "lumber industry was reinvigorated in Wallowa County in 1946 when the Mt. Emily Lumber Company moved one of their mills to Enterprise, and began logging in the Chesnimnus District of the Wallowa National Forest. The company had begun buying timber in the area during the 1930s and 1940s, and there was enough to justify the mill."

The Mt. Emily Lumber Company expanded their mill in October 1947 when it started operating a new band sawmill. A second shift opened in the spring of 1950, but the sawmill was closed in November 1953. In early 1955, Mt. Emily Lumber was sold to the Valsetz Lumber Company, and became the Templeton Lumber Company. The company was bought by Boise Cascade in 1960. Today, little remains of the large lumber mill that was once at Enterprise. The mill pond and a few storage sheds still exist just north of the tracks and a block west of Depot Street.

78.5 WALLOWA RIVER BRIDGE – It actually takes three separate bridges to cross the Wallowa River here, since the river really wanders in this area. The bridges are at 78.2 (single-span timber pile trestle), 78.3 (two-span timber pile trestle), and 78.5 (three-span timber pile trestle).

The railroad has turned south to head from Enterprise to Joseph. In this area, the railroad is crossing a wide floodplain with a number of small channels that are wet even during the dry season. The railroad is heading uphill on grades as much as 1.5%.

The territory between Enterprise and Joseph is the most developed part of the line except for the La Grande-Island City area. This area has a great deal of farming and irrigation canals run throughout the valley, feeding the various farms water from the snowmelt on the nearby Wallowa Mountains. The railroad crosses several small irrigation ditches using small timber spans.

82.2 JOSEPH STATE AIRPORT – The railroad crosses Russell Lane. To the west (railroad-south) is the Joseph State Airport, owned by the Oregon Department of Aviation. Located at an elevation of 4121 feet, the airport sees about ten uses a day, all private planes as there is no regular commercial passenger service. The Joseph State Airport is somewhat unique in that it does not have an IATA (International Air Transport Association) three-letter location identifier. This is the three letters used to identify an airport, the same three letters you see on your luggage tag when you check your bags. Generally, airports have the same identifier assigned by both IATA and the Federal Aviation Administration (FAA). However, the FAA assigned Joseph the letters JSY, which IATA uses for the Syros Island National Airport on Syros Island in Greece.

Union Pacific used to have several tracks in this area, including several spur tracks to the south (compass-west) and a siding to the north (compass-east). This was the Joseph Forest Products wood-treating facility, which operated at the site from 1974 until 1985 when a fire destroyed the treatment building. During the fire and possibly before, an estimated 200 gallons of concentrated treatment paste and about 3000 gallons of treatment solution were lost. The treatment was a water-based chromated copper arsenate preservative.

Because of the soil contamination, the Environmental Protection Agency (EPA) became involved and conducted a cleanup of the site. The process included "excavation and off-site disposal of contaminated soil and debris; demolition of the on-site treatment building; decontamination of the drip pad and treatment equipment; excavation and decontamination of underground storage tanks; removal and disposal of asbestos; implementation of institutional controls and groundwater monitoring for a period of two years." This work took place in 1991 and 1993, and the site was removed from the EPA Superfund program's National Priorities List (NPL) in 1999. Today the site is the open land south of Russell Lane between the railroad and the airport.

82.9 WALLOWA RIVER BRIDGE – The railroad crosses the Wallowa River for the last time on a 5-span timber pile trestle. The tracks also make a sharp 8-degree turn to the northeast, changing the direction of travel by almost 120 degrees, or one-third of a full circle. Union Pacific once had a long spur track just east of the bridge that served the sawmill complex to the south.

The Timber Industry at Joseph

The Wallowa River was an attraction for sawmills along its entire length, and it was no different at Joseph. The first major lumber mill at Joseph was the A. M. Hall & Son Joseph Planing Mill, located on the banks of the Wallowa River near here. This area between the railroad's Wallowa River bridge and the tall grain elevator has historically been filled with sawmills.

The Timberman of October 1912, in their report on the railroad's Elgin-Joseph Branch, listed a number of lumber mills in the region, but only two local facilities. The first was the custom planing mill of Harry Carpenter. The second was the operation of the Dawson Brothers. They operated a planing mill and lumber yard, supported by their sawmill located 12 miles from Joseph. The article also stated that mills in the area produced "about two and a half million feet annually" and that "between three and four hundred thousand is shipped by rail; the balance is consumed locally."

The early years at Joseph saw several small mills built, burned and then rebuilt. However, it wasn't until after World War II that a major mill was built. This process began when J. Herbert Bate bought the sawmill at Joseph at the same time that they bought the Bowman-Hicks mill in Wallowa. At the time, the Mt. Joseph Pine Company went through several owners, and the mill was finally sold to the Pondosa Pine

Lumber Company at Elgin in 1947. With this purchase, plans were immediately announced to spend $100,000 to build a new, more modern mill. However, in June 1949, Pondosa Pine's Joseph Mill was destroyed by fire.

To replace the burned mill, construction on a new mill began near the Joseph airport. Over the next several decades, the mills in the area were expanded, cut back, modernized, closed, re-opened, and torn down. These patterns very much followed the national economic and construction trends. Some of the newspaper headlines can be used to tell the story, such as "Boise Cascade to end planer ops at Joseph" (December 5, 1963); "Ch. Joseph Lumber Co. to expand mill" (November 11, 1965); "Joseph Boise Cascade to add third shift" (August 29, 1974); and "Boise Cascade mill at Joseph to drop one shift" (May 24, 1979).

By the late 1970s, W L Forest Industries was operating the Joseph mill, which they closed in 1985, and then sold to Sequoia Forest Products (1985). Within a decade, the mill belonged to RY Timber (1986), and then Thebault-Krieger (1995), which renamed it the Joseph Timber Company. The mill finally closed in 2002, and its remains were removed several years later. Although the mill was closed, the timberlands remained. For example, in 2017, RY Timber announced that it was selling 20,000 acres of private land in the area, exiting the Oregon timber market and concentrating on its Montana operations.

Boise Cascade at Joseph

Thanks to several Oregon Department of Environmental Quality reports, information about the Boise Cascade facility is readily available. Boise Cascade at one time filled the space west of the Joseph Rodeo Grounds, between the Wallowa River and the railroad. They also used the space west of the railroad wye to Samples Drive. During the 1980s, Union Pacific's Joseph Branch passed right through the middle of this property.

The property had been used for many years by sawmills. During the late 1940s, two sawmills still existed here, and they were bought by Boise Cascade during the 1950s. This mill was for the most part simply a basic sawmill. Planer operations ended here late in 1963. The mill added and subtracted shifts during the 1970s based upon demand, and then began a slow slide during the 1980s as the age of the mill and the available timber made it less competitive. A strike at the mill in 1988 didn't help things, and Boise Cascade closed their Joseph sawmill in 1994.

The area north of the tracks between the railroad wye and Samples Drive was the Boise Cascade mill yard, used for log storage. Much of this property is now used by JayZee Lumber. This company specializes in custom milling of logs obtained from sustainable wood sources in the area. They can reproduce custom beams for building restoration projects, for a new timber frame home, or for almost any special project.

Between the tracks and the Wallowa River was the heart of the old Boise Cascade sawmill. Located where cars park today north of where Airport Lane bridges over the Wallowa River, was once the log pond, filled from the adjacent river. On the west side of the log pond was the sawmill, with its sorting shed further to the west. There was also a lunch room, chip loader, cooling shed, and other buildings on the property. Log trucks would enter the property next to the railroad off of Russell Street, passing north of the corrals that are a part of the rodeo grounds. They would then drop their logs in the log yard to the north and east of the log pond. A garage with gasoline and diesel fuel was located on the north side of the log yard.

Logs went through the pond for cleaning, and then the sawmill and sorter. Finished lumber went to the west lumber yard alongside the tracks for shipment by rail and truck. Chips from the production facility were stored and then loaded at a facility on the southwest part of the property, directly adjacent to the Wallowa River. Today, the property has been cleaned and a few sheds and foundations are all that remain.

83.3 JOSEPH (J) – As stated in the October 1912 report on the Elgin-Joseph Branch in *The Timberman*, "Joseph, at an elevation of 4,140 feet, is the terminus of the Elgin Branch of the O. W. R. & N Railroad, 86 miles from La Grande, in the famous Wallowa Valley, rich in soil timber and natural scenery. Wallowa Lake is a most beautiful sheet of water, nestling at the foot of the eternal snow-clad Blue Mountains, with their wooded sides sloping to the water's edge, forming a picture of surpassing grandeur and beauty. The lake is five miles long, a mile wide with depths of over 400 feet. The Wallowa Lake is fed by the two branches of the Wallowa River. Five irrigation ditches tap the lake, carrying the water to the fertile valley lands. This is an ideal stock and grain section."

Joseph sits at the top of a rail climb of about 1.5%, reaching an elevation of 4142 feet above sea level. As with many towns, Joseph didn't keep its original name. The area was called Hah-um-sah-pah by area Natives. After looking around, you will probably agree that the name was appropriate as it means "big rocks lying scattered around." As a town began to grow here, the names of Lake City and Silver City were originally proposed for the community. However, due to other towns also having these names, postal officials refused to accept either name. Therefore, in 1880, the community became known as Joseph, honoring the father and son chiefs of the Wallowa Band of the Nez Percé tribe.

Matthew Johnson was the first postmaster in Joseph, operating it out of his small general store. Evidently much of the early business in the area involved livestock or farming as the first two major businesses that opened were blacksmiths, separately operated by Ryer Olsen and Robert Olsen. By 1881, Joseph had a mercantile store, a mill, and a schoolhouse. The first newspaper opened in 1883 as *The Chieftain*, but it relocated to Enterprise in 1893. In 1887, Joseph was platted and incorporated, and also named as the first county seat of Wallowa County (although it was moved to Enterprise in 1888). The construction of a waterworks system was authorized in 1888, and electric lights arrived in 1900.

Joseph's economy has traditionally been based upon the land. Farming, ranching and timber have created a series of boom and bust cycles. In 1900, Joseph had 237 residents. After the railroad arrived in 1908, the number climbed to more than 800. The typical general stores, hotels and restaurants, doctor offices, drug stores and other business were also soon open. The potential for area agriculture caused the Union Pacific to operate one of their agricultural improvement trains to Joseph in 1909, the first harvest season after the rails arrived in town. This train included two business/coach cars, three baggage cars with displays and classrooms, three flat cars with displays of farming machinery, a stock car and a caboose.

All of this was pulled by a small steamer with what appears to be a 2-6-0 wheel arrangement.

The 1910s and early 1920s were good to Joseph, but it did not last. For example, the National Register of Historic Places reported that a limited number of substantial buildings were built in Joseph about the time the railroad arrived, but few after that time until more modern times. Even those that were built suffered during the 1920s. For example, the First National Bank of Joseph closed its doors June 1, 1923. The National Register cited the June 7, 1923, issue of the *Enterprise Record Chieftain*, which reported "With the First National Bank of Joseph, it was not a question of insolvency, as the paper assets were fully adequate, but of expansion and 'frozen' credits, notes which could not be paid when due." The National Register report stated that "this resulted from a great depreciation in values of stock and land since the inflation of post World War I times. Values depreciated so much, particularly cattle values, that the bank could not carry the load. Stockmen had nothing but losses and no means to pay their notes." The bank building became the post office in 1925.

By the 1930s, the population of Joseph had declined and a number of the storefronts along Main Street were empty. Three of these buildings still stand and are listed on the National Register of Historic Places. Located just north of First Street is the First National Bank of Joseph, with the Dr. J. W. Barnard Building built adjacent at the same time as part of the same construction project. Both buildings were built in 1908 by contractor Frank Marr. Dr. Jerome W. Barnard had the building constructed for his Joseph Drug Company, which operated a drug store and soda fountain. Dr. Barnard was also part of the Black Marble & Lime Company, located southeast of Enterprise.

The third building is the former First Bank of Joseph building, now the home of the Wallowa County Museum, located at the corner of Second and Main in downtown Joseph. The bank moved out in 1914 and the building became the office and operating room of Dr. Verdo Gregory. The building became the property of the City of Joseph in 1927, and it was used as a community center, meeting room and performing arts theater. The building was also used as the city hall and library.

There was some recovery during the late 1930s, but it was the late 1940s before some of the lost businesses were replaced. Because of this, the National Register commented that the downtown business district shows little change from this earlier era. The big change in Joseph came about during the 1990s and later as much of the timber industry went away and tourism became the dominant economic force in the community. Today's tourism includes the arts, in particular bronze castings and sculptures, giving Joseph the name of Oregon's Bronze Capital. This is actually the second tourism boom, and more on the subject is covered below.

The Josephs of the Nez Percé

Joseph, and the nearby Wallowa Lake, was once the heart of the ancestral homeland of the Nimiipuu, or Nez Percé. The name Joseph has much importance in the area, and with the Nez Percé. The problem for many is that they do not recognize that there were actually two chiefs of the Nez Percé by the name Joseph, and they were father and son.

The father was known as Old Chief Joseph or Joseph the Elder. In 1855, Joseph the Elder helped the govenor of the Territory of Washington establish a Nez Percé reservation that stretched from Oregon into Idaho. This included the Wallowa Valley that the City of Joseph sits in today. Joseph the Elder was known to be friendly to whites, and even ordered that they be protected when they encroached upon the property of the Nez Percé. The plan lasted until gold was discovered in the area in 1863. To make the gold finds available to miners, the federal government took back almost six million acres of this land, leaving the Nez Percé on a reservation in Idaho that was only one tenth the reservation's original size. However, Joseph refused the change, and destroyed his American flag and his Bible. He also refused to sign the agreement or to lead his Wallowa band out of the Wallowa Valley.

When Joseph the Elder died in 1871, Joseph the Younger was chosen to succeed him. Joseph the Younger, Hin-mah-too-yah-lat-kekt or "Thunder Rolling Down the Mountain," had been educated at a mission school, and knew English and many of the laws of the United States. Even with violent conflict underway, he worked for a peaceful solution. In 1873, a federal order gave the Wallowa Valley back to the tribe and ordered all whites to be removed. However, further political and legal action reversed the ruling, and the tribe was again ordered to leave the area. General Oliver Otis Howard brought a calvary force to the valley in early 1877 to force out the Wallowa band. Raids by both parties led to violence and Joseph the Younger led his band on a more than one-thousand-mile march across Oregon, Washington, Idaho, and Montana, trying to avoid the pursuing troops. After a series of battles, the group almost reached the Canadian border before surrendering to General Nelson A. Miles in the Bear Paw mountains of Montana. On October 5, 1877, Chief Joseph ended his efforts, stating "Hear me, my chiefs; my heart is sick and sad. From where the Sun now stands, I will fight no more forever."

While Joseph the Younger lost his war, he gained a great deal of support, even from the white settlers in the region. He treated prisoners humanely, he purchased supplies from ranchers and storekeepers rather than stealing them, and he is credited with protecting women, children, and the elderly, both white and Indian. However, Joseph and the survivors were sent to Indian Territory in today's Oklahoma, where many died. In 1885, they were allowed to move to a new reservation in Washington State. Until he died in 1904, Joseph the Younger continued his fight for respect and justice, including visits with President Theodore Roosevelt. His reputation, and that of his father, led to the use of their name for the City of Joseph, Oregon.

The Development of Tourism at Joseph

Tourism in the Wallowa area began long before white settlers entered the region. For generations, members of the Wallowa band of the Nez Percé and others visited the area for the hunting and fishing. The area south of Joseph is a transition zone between the high valley (5000 feet above sea level) and the rugged mountains further to the south. These mountains are the magnificent Wallowa Mountains, some reaching over 10,000 feet.

The Wallowa Mountains have also been known as the Blue, the Granite, and the Eagle Mountains. The Lewis and Clark map of 1805-1806 shows them as the Wallowa Mountains. The mountains are unique in Oregon because of their granite nature, unlike the volcanic nature throughout the rest of the state. These mountains include glaciers and a number of wild rivers. Directly south of Joseph is Chief Joseph Mountain (also known at times as Tunnel Mountain and Point Joseph – it was officially named Chief Joseph Mountain in 1925 by the United States Board on Geographic Names). Just to its west is Sawtooth Peak (9173 feet) and Twin Peaks (9671 feet). To the south of these mountains can be found Matterhorn (at 10,004 feet, it was named for the Matterhorn in Switzerland), in the area where Hurricane Creek and the East Lostine Rivers start.

To the south of Wallowa Lake is a wall of mountains that provide the source of moisture for the West and East Forks of the Wallowa River. This wall includes Craig Mountain (9202 feet – named for "Pap" Craig, a pioneer resident of the county and former county sheriff and judge), Petes Point (9675 feet – named for Peter Beaudoin, once one of the largest sheep owners in eastern Oregon), and Aneroid Mountain (9702 feet). Aneroid Mountain, as well as nearby Aneroid Lake, were reportedly named by Hoffman Philip in 1897 while on a mapping trip for the U.S. Fish Commission. He named both land features for the aneroid barometer he used to determine elevations at that time. However, some argue that it is a misspelling of Anna Royal or Anna Royl, both reportedly used for a while at about the same time. These names come from several early residents of the area, or friends of residents, but people can't agree on either. A good map will show that the area includes the Wallowa and Whitman National Forests, as well as the Eagle Cap Wilderness area.

To the south of Lake Wallowa is a wall of mountains and wilderness, attracting tourists year round. Photo by Barton Jennings.

These mountains quickly attracted tourists, especially during the summer when the area would still remain cool. Wallowa Lake was originally named Spalding Lake in 1830 for Presbyterian missionary H. H. Spalding. The lake was also named Silver Lake and then Joseph Lake before Wallowa Lake was settled upon. By the late 1800s, the lake had already become a resort area with boat tours and special excursions. By 1900, there were horse and cabin rentals and a resort hotel. With the arrival of the railroad in Joseph in 1908 came the Wallowa Lake Amusement Park, a collection of restaurants, stores, bowling alley, dance hall, an 80-seat tour boat, a laundry, outdoor movie theater, a horse-powered carousel, and a lot more cabins.

Expansion of the facility pretty much ended after World War I (except for the Wallowa Lake Lodge built in 1923). The popularity of the site peaked in the 1930s and then began to falter, as did much of the area business. To try to save part of what was here, the

Wallowa Lake State Park was established in 1946. A slow recovery began in the 1960s with a huge boom over the last several decades.

The state park now features camper hook-ups, tent locations, a marina, picnic grounds, and many other facilities. Also at the south end of Wallowa Lake are a number of private resorts, camps, homes, riding stables, and other facilities, reminding many of a Swiss alpine village. A major attraction is the Wallowa Lake Tramway, opened in 1970 and lifting people 3700 feet to the top of Mt. Howard at more than 8200 feet. There is also access to hundreds of miles of hiking trails.

North of the lake and just south of town is the Iwetemlaykin State Heritage Site, adjacent to the Old Chief Joseph Gravesite and Cemetery. This area is a Nez Percé National Historical Park, and is considered to be a sacred place to the Nez Percé Tribe, the Confederated Tribes of the Colville Reservation, and the Confederated Tribes of the Umatilla Indian Reservation. "Iwetemlaykin" (ee-weh-TEMM-lye-kinn) is the Nez Percé name for the Wallowa Lake area, and translates to "at the edge of the lake." This location may be part of the original area's tourism that dates back centuries.

Today's Joseph, Oregon

Joseph is again booming as a tourist destination. Efforts by the community have made the town a destination all year long. January features the Annual Eagle Cap Extreme Sled Dog Race, featuring 22, 62, 100- and 200-mile races, with the 200-mile race being Oregon's only Iditarod and Yukon Quest Qualifier. Outdoor events last all year with hiking, biking and a number of other activities. July features the Chief Joseph Days Rodeo; the Bronze, Blues and Brews event is in August; and Alpenfest, a Swiss-Bavarian festival, is held in September.

Downtown has also changed and become a major draw, and a walk around town will find the large number of bronze statues produced locally, many hanging flower boxes, and about the cleanest town in the country. Art galleries and craft stores now fill what were once a number of empty storefronts.

Tennis great Margaret Evelyn Osborne, later Margaret Osbourne duPont, who won a record twenty-five Grand Slams at the U.S. Championships, was born in Joseph in 1918. She was ranked number one in the world for many years, with most of her Grand Slam titles playing women's doubles. She also won more mixed doubles titles at the U.S. Championships than any other player.

In 1940, Actor Walter Brennan bought the 12,000-acre Lightning Creek Ranch, located twenty miles south of Joseph. He soon became a leader in the town and built the Indian Lodge Motel, a movie theater and a variety store. His hotel has been restored and is still open to guests. Walter Brennan Days are celebrated in Joseph in late April of each year, and some of his family still live in the area.

Alvin M. Josephy, Jr., also has close ties to the community. Josephy was an American historian who specialized in Native American issues, and has been called the "leading non-Indian writer about Native Americans." Josephy worked as a Hollywood screenwriter and newspaper correspondent before serving as a United States Marine Corps combat correspondent during World War II, being awarded the Bronze Star Medal for his coverage of the invasion of Guam. Alvin and his wife Betty bought a ranch near Joseph and used it as a camp for Nez Percé children. His collection of books and papers became the basis for the Josephy Library, which also operates as a regional arts and culture center.

Joseph is still a small town with a population of 1081 in the 2010 census. However, this is the largest number of residents the city has ever had. Besides tourism, area ranching and some farming and timber production are still supported by the community.

Joseph and the Railroad

In 1908, the Oregon Railroad & Navigation Company completed their branch line to Joseph. Almost immediately, train service began, highlighted by passenger trains #31 and #32. #31 operated from Joseph (8:00am as of October 12, 1909), arriving at La Grande at 2:15pm. #32 departed La Grande at 9:45am and arrived at Joseph at 4:00pm. Both trains operated daily.

Little changed over the next decade except the train numbers and a bit of the timing. The October 11, 1925, schedule had train #42 departing La Grande at 10:30am and arriving at Joseph at 2:20pm. The train returned as train #41, leaving Joseph at 2:40pm and arriving back at La Grande at 6:10pm. The schedule was closely timed with mainline trains to and from Portland, Oregon. This basic schedule continued for many years. For example, in 1948 when the train was a mixed passenger and freight train, a passenger would pretty much have to spend the night to see much of Joseph as train #304 was scheduled to arrive at 11:15am and then depart back toward La Grande at 12:45pm, giving just 90 minutes for the crew to switch the several industries here and have lunch. Over the years, some schedules had the train laying over in Joseph at night, but the community never had much of a shop or locomotive facility.

The track never went further than Joseph, so both the grain and timber industries located here. Photo by Barton Jennings.

However, there were a number of other rail facilities here. For the steam locomotives, there was a water column using Joseph city water as a source. There was also a 50-ton coal timber platform here, the only source of coal on the Joseph Branch. A wye track also was here to turn locomotives and trains as needed. Besides the depot and freight house, there was a freight platform. There was also a 7-pen stockyard for the livestock.

The original Joseph Depot was essentially the same as the ones at Wallowa and Enterprise, about 21 feet wide and 64 feet long with a gambrel roof over the second story. Eventually, a long freight room was added to one end of the structure, replacing a separate building.

Joseph has also become the home of the Joseph Branch Railriders, one of a number of companies across the country that offer rail bike rides on actual railroads. The firm has been running trips since 2014. The company offers Joseph to Enterprise and Minam to Wallowa roundtrips on select dates.

83.6 END OF BRANCH – The line ends just past the retired Wallowa County Grain Growers elevator. The last of the construction on the Joseph Branch occurred in 1927 when the line was extended to reach a new grain elevator.

The Wallowa County Grain Growers elevator towers over the Eagle Cap Excursion Train at Joseph, Oregon. Photo by Barton Jennings.

Sitting in the middle of the wye near the end of the line is the tallest building in Joseph, the old grain elevator. Note the Wallowa County Grain Growers name painted near the base. The Wallowa County

Grain Growers was formed in 1944 to serve the Wallowa County area, but has since expanded to include facilities (including the local John Deere dealerships) in La Grande and Baker, Oregon.

About the Author

For almost three decades, Barton Jennings has been organizing charter passenger trains and writing the route descriptions, both for planning purposes and for the enjoyment of the passengers. These trips have been from coast to coast, often covering operations that haven't seen a passenger train in decades. In addition, he has written a number of articles about various railroads for rail hobby magazines. His basement has several rooms full of books, timetables and other documents about this and other railroads – important research items from a time long before today's internet. Today, Bart Jennings, after years working in the railroad industry, is a professor of supply chain management and teaches transportation operations. He also still teaches regulatory issues for the railroad industry, a way to stay in touch with the industry he loves. The writing of this book was a particularly fond activity, getting to relive the time when he managed the track maintenance on the branch, and later operated several charter trains between Joseph and Gulling. During 1985-1986, Bart was the Union Pacific Roadmaster, based in LaGrande, who had responsibility for the Joseph Branch.

Made in the USA
Lexington, KY
29 September 2019